Afghans to Knit & Crochet

Also by Leslie Linsley

Quick and Easy Knit & Crochet

Custom Made

Fabulous Furniture Decorations

Wildcrafts

The Decoupage Workshop

Scrimshaw

Decoupage: A New Look at an Old Craft

Decoupage for Young Crafters

Decoupage on . . .

Army Navy Surplus: A Decorating Source

Photocraft

New Ideas for Old Furniture

The Great Bazaar

Making It Personal with Monograms, Initials and Names

Air Crafts

Million Dollar Projects from the 5 & 10¢ Store

Christmas Ornaments and Stockings

America's Favorite Quilts

Afghans
to Knit & Crochet

Leslie Linsley

ST. MARTIN'S
MAREK

Afghans to Knit & Crochet

Preparation and design: Jon Aron Studio

Art direction:	Jon Aron
Research:	Amy Brunhuber
Illustrations:	Greg Worth
Photography:	Jon Aron
Craft contributors:	Anna Beck
	Marilyn Berthelette
	Elizabeth Cherniak
	Enid Cherniak
	Anne Dyer
	Bee Gonella
	Evelyn Hochman
	Lee Holmes
	Sylvia Kaplan
	Ruth Linsley
	Helen Millman
	Robin Marie Murray
	Sylvia Rinaudo
	Helen Rochlin
	Lori Scamporino
	Roberta Sohmer

Projects on pages 38, 46, and 87 designed by Bee Gonella

AFGHANS TO KNIT AND CROCHET. Copyright © 1984 by Leslie Linsley. All rights reserved. Printed in the United States of America. No part of this book may be used or reproduced in any manner whatsoever without written permission except in the case of brief quotations embodied in critical articles or reviews. For information, address St. Martin's Press, 175 Fifth Avenue, New York, N.Y. 10010.

Library of Congress Cataloging in Publication Data
Linsley, Leslie.
   Afghans to knit and crochet.

   1. Afghans (Coverlets) 2. Knitting. 3. Crocheting.
1. Title.
TT825.L56   1984   746.9′7041   83-21129
ISBN 0-312-00930-5

First Edition
10 9 8 7 6 5 4 3 2 1

I am especially grateful to Bee Gonella for her invaluable input, both technical and creative, throughout the production of this book, and to my mother, Ruth Linsley, who kept everyone knitting and in good spirits.

I would like to thank the needleworkers who patiently worked the designs for each afghan, making corrections and suggestions all the way.

My appreciation is also extended to the yarn manufacturers and distributors who have been helpful in the preparation of this book. Their cooperation and interest in furnishing the beautiful materials for the purpose of designing the projects have been most generous. They are:

Bernat Yarn and Craft Corp., Uxbridge, Massachusetts
Bucilla, New York, New York
Coats & Clark, Inc., Stamford, Connecticut
Phildar, Inc., Norcross, Georgia
The Settlement Farm, Cambridge, Vermont
Tahki Imports Ltd., Hackensack, New Jersey

L.L.

for my grandmother, Anna Zuckerman

Contents

Afghans to Knit & Crochet

Introduction

I don't know anyone who didn't grow up with an afghan in the house. Most of the "heirloom" afghans seem to be composed of a multitude of colors, testifying to the practicality of the needleworker. My favorite, which I have had since childhood, looks like a patchwork quilt. Most of the background is black since the granny squares are joined with borders of this color. But the overall colors blend in a nondescript pattern. Colors start and stop at random, such being the nature of a project made from scraps.

We always had a zigzag or chevron striped cover folded at the end of a bed, and the couch held another afghan thrown invitingly over the back. I suppose knitters and crocheters have passed on much of their handiwork to children, grandchildren, and friends. Can there be a nicer expression of caring?

Making something by hand has become more important than ever and a handmade gift more prized. Especially in our high tech society, it is extremely important to create something unique. In this way we pass along something of ourselves and the time we live in. Most of all, it is an expression or statement that we can create something worthwhile.

The value of a handmade afghan goes beyond its serviceability. Imagine your first baby wrapped in a blanket that you, your mother, or your grandmother lovingly made. Each stitch is an anticipation of the event to come. The hours of needlework are part of the process. Years after the baby is grown, the blanket may still endure.

Leaving home with a handmade afghan can make the college student or new bride feel like she is taking part of her family with her. What could be more comforting than wrapping oneself in an afghan from home?

There are many reasons why an afghan is a wonderful project for the needleworker. Everyone loves afghans. Perhaps it's because of the endless color and pattern combinations, the variety of textures, and because they will last forever. Afghans make wonderful gifts, they are practical and warm, and they provide hours of relaxation and enjoyment. Most afghan projects are portable and can be made in pieces, then put together for the final step. Best of all, these projects need no fitting.

The yarns available today make an afghan project that much more enjoyable than ever before. There is so much to choose from and a project can be as simple or extravagant as the craftworker wants to make it.

The afghans presented here are made with a variety of yarn and color combinations. Where expensive yarns were used, less expensive material that can be used to produce the same effect is alway suggested.

Sizes are given for each project with directions for enlarging or decreasing to suit your needs. I think you'll find enough variety to make you want to do several. The stitches used in all projects are basic. There are no fancy or complicated stitches although a few projects are designed for the more experienced needleworker. However, most were created for quick and easy crafting. I think you'll find them all rewarding and enjoyable to make.

Getting started in knitting

Knitting is based on learning how to do two basic stitches, knit and purl. From these you can make all kinds of knitted projects. By combining these two stitches in different variations, such as 2 knit, 2 purl, or 1 row of knit and 1 row of purl, you will be able to create a simple garment or as elaborate a project as you can imagine.

As a beginner, you will find that most of the projects in this book confine themselves to a basic knit and purl stitch to produce what is known as a stockinette pattern. This is the most popular stitch combination and is easy to learn. If you are a practiced knitter, you'll find a variety of projects that introduce new ideas and combinations of yarn that will make them enjoyable to do. Best of all, the projects are quick and easy, but the results should be rewardingly professional looking.

The following will teach you what you need to know in order to make the knitting projects in this book. You will also be able to go on to create your own designs or variations on the original patterns.

Casting on

To begin any project, you will need to cast a specified number of stitches onto your needles. This becomes the base from which you will work your first row of knitting. When counting rows, do not count the cast-on row.

1. Start by making a slip knot, leaving a tail of yarn about 3 inches long. Place the loop of the knot on the left-hand needle. (For left-handers, reverse these and all other instructions.) Use your right-hand needle to make the stitches to cast onto the left-hand needle as follows.

2. Wrap the yarn around your left forefinger to create tension, and insert the right-hand needle from front to back through the loop on the left-hand needle. The two needles are now in the loop, with the right-hand needle behind the left.

3. Bring the yarn clockwise around the right-hand needle. With the right-hand needle, pull the yarn through the loop on the left needle.

4. Bring the tip of the left-hand needle from right to left through the loop on the right needle.

5. Withdraw the right-hand needle, pull the yarn slightly taut, and you have 2 stitches on the left needle. Continue to do this until you have the number of stitches needed.

casting on

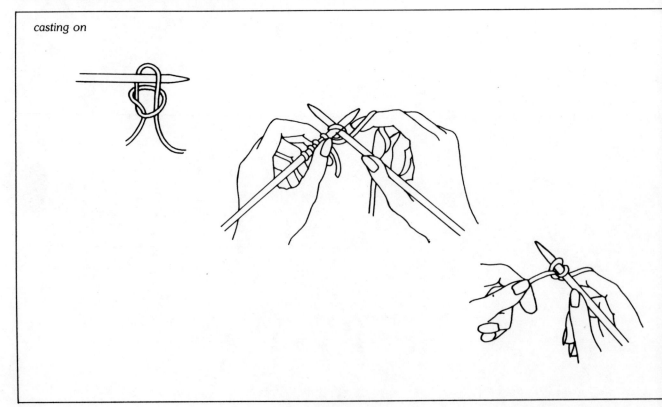

Knit stitch

A project worked with all knitting stitches is called a garter-stitch fabric.

1. Hold the needle with cast-on stitches in your left hand, with the yarn around your left forefinger. Insert the right-hand needle from front to back through the first loop on the left-hand needle.

2. Bring the yarn under and over the point of the right needle. Draw the yarn through the loop with the point of the needle.

3. Use your right forefinger to push the tip of the left needle down, to let the loop on the left needle slip off. You now have one stitch on your right needle. Work across the row in this way.

After finishing a row of knitting, transfer the right-hand needle to left hand and the left to the right, turning the needles also (the points always face each other), and continue the next row in the same way, always taking the stitches from the left to the right needle.

When you have practiced making nice neat rows at an even tension, you can turn this garter stitch into a project.

garter stitch fabric

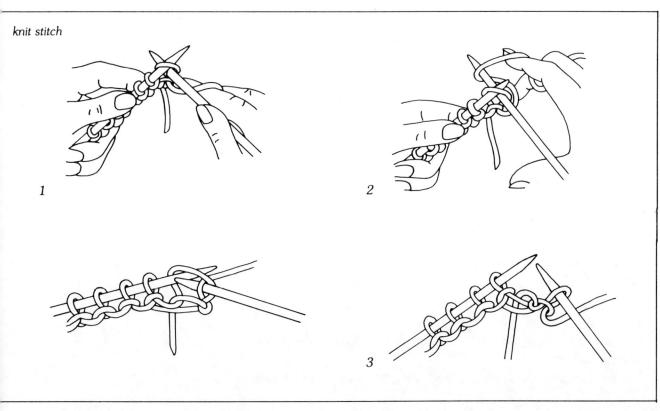

knit stitch

1

2

3

Purl stitch

1. With cast-on stitches on your left-hand needle, insert the point of your right-hand needle from right to left through the *front* of the first stitch. With the yarn in front of your work (rather than in back as with the knit stitch), wind it over and around the needle's point.
2. Draw the yarn back through the stitch and let the loop on the left needle slip off the needle. Your first purl stitch is now on your right-hand needle.

Stockinette stitch

Work one row with the knit stitch. Purl each stitch in the next row. Continue to knit one row and purl the next for a stockinette fabric. The pattern on the front of the work is that of interlocking V's. The back of the fabric looks like a tighter version of all garter stitch (knit).

Increasing a stitch

This means that you will be making two stitches from one on a row. Knit the first stitch as usual, but do not drop the stitch off the left-hand needle. Bring the right-hand needle behind the left needle and insert it from right to left into the back of the same stitch. Make another stitch by winding yarn under and over the right-hand needle (knit stitch). Slip the stitch off the left-hand needle.

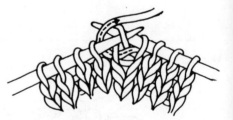

If you are increasing a stitch on a purl row, purl the first stitch but do not slip it off. Bring the yarn between the needles to the back of the work, and knit a stitch in back of the same stitch unless otherwise instructed.

Decreasing a stitch

If you are decreasing stitches, to shape a raglan armhole, for example, you will be knitting or purling two stitches together to form one stitch. In a pattern direction this will be given as k 2 tog or p 2 tog.

On the right side of your work, knit 2 stitches together as if they were one. If worked through the front of the stitches, the decrease slants to the right; if through the back of the stitches, it slants to the left.

When decreasing a purl stitch, work on the wrong side and purl 2 stitches together.

Psso means pass slip stitch over and is another way of decreasing a stitch. You slip the first stitch by taking it onto the right-hand needle from the left without knitting it, keeping the yarn in back of the work. Knit the next stitch and bring the slip stitch over the knit stitch as you would when binding off. (When slipping a stitch in a purl row, keep the yarn in front of the work.)

Binding off

1. Knit the first two stitches. Insert the left-hand needle from left to right through the front of the first (the right-most) stitch.
2. Lift the first stitch over the second stitch and the tip of the right-hand needle. (Use your left hand to push the tip of the right-hand needle back while pulling the stitch through.) Let the lifted stitch drop, and you now have one stitch on the right-hand needle. Knit another stitch and lift the right-most stitch over the next as before. Repeat this across the row until one stitch is left.
3. Loosen the remaining loop on the right-hand needle and withdraw the needle. Cut the yarn, leaving 2 or 3 inches (unless the instructions for your project specify a longer tail), and pull this tail through the loop. Tighten the knot.

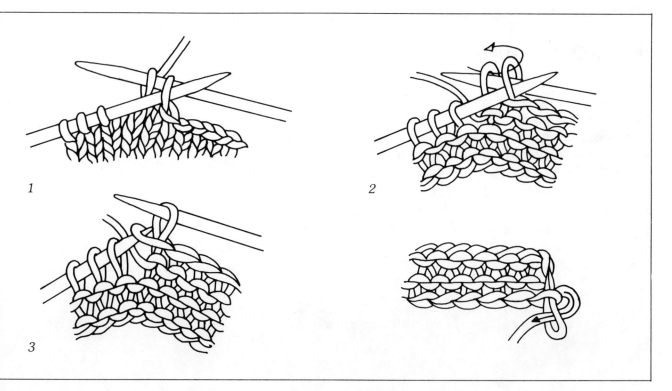

1

2

3

Cable stitches

Cable stitches are often used in fisherman knit and to add interest to a plain project.

Producing a cable twist requires the use of a double-pointed cable needle. This should be the same size or slightly smaller than those used to knit the afghan.

Determine where the cable stitch will be and begin on the right side of the work. Purl across until you come to the point where the cable will begin. Using the cable needle. place one end from right to left through the next stitch. Allow this stitch to slip off the left-hand needle (reverse for left-handed people). Repeat for the next two stitches. With the three stitches on the cable needle, keep it at the front of the work. Ignoring this needle, take the yarn to the back of the work and knit the next three stitches with the other two needles as usual.

Next, hold the cable needle with your left hand and push the stitches to the right side of the needle. Using the right-hand needle and the cable needle, knit the three stitches on the cable needle. Purl to the end of the row. Work the straight rows between cable twists according to the directions for each project. Always twist your cable on the right side. The cable will have tighter or looser twists depending on the number of rows between twists. The fewer the rows between twists, the tighter the cable pattern.

Joining new yarn

Always join new yarn at the beginning of a row. If you get partway across and run out of yarn, pull out stitches to the beginning of the row and add the new yarn. (This is to avoid knots in the middle of a piece.) Insert the right-hand needle into the first stitch on the left-hand needle. Wrap the new yarn around the right-hand needle, leaving a tail as you did when starting your work. Pull the right-hand needle through the first stitch and continue to knit as before. Pull the side strands of yarn to tighten. Use these to attach pieces of the project being worked, or weave them into the project later.

Knitting tips

Yarn

There are hundreds of yarns to choose from, and each has its best uses. Most patterns recommend the best yarn for the project. If the brand name is not given, the yarn group usually is. This might be a bulky weight, worsted, sportyarn, etc. If you are substituting yarns for those given in a pattern, be sure that the weight is similar. Look for a yarn with the same gauge. This information is usually found on the label of the yarn.

Often the yarn looks quite different, when it is made up, from what it looked like on the skein. It's a good idea, especially when using expensive yarn or when making a large project, to buy only one skein and make a swatch. In this way you can see what the knitted yarn will look like before making the investment of time and money. Then buy enough yarn needed for a project. Often colors change from one dye lot to another and you may have trouble matching yarns later on if you run out.

Gauge

The gauge is the number of stitches and number of rows per inch you knit with the yarn and needles recommended. The gauge is the tension at which you work, and this determines the size of the project. This is especially important when making a garment to wear. If your gauge doesn't match the gauge given with the pattern, the garment won't fit as stated.

Before beginning any project, test your gauge by making a swatch using the yarn and needles recommended. Knit in the stitch pattern for a 4×4-inch square. Check the gauge given and mark the number of stitches with pins. For example, if the gauge calls for 7 stitches to 2 inches, count 7 stitches in the middle of the work and mark where they begin and end. With a tape measure check to see what the measurement is for 7 stitches. If the 7 stitches make less than 2 inches, your gauge is too tight. Make another sample with needles a size larger. If the 7 stitches measure more than 2 inches, you will need to go down a size with your needles. Sometimes the gauge difference occurs because the yarn used is not exactly what is recommended in the directions.

count stitches per inch for gauge

count rows per inch for gauge

Blocking

Many of the afghans require blocking after they are finished. This means squaring them off to the correct size and shape.

Different yarns are treated differently, and this is why it's important to keep the labels from your yarn to refer to after the knitting has been completed. Sometimes the label gives blocking directions, but if not, you will need the information concerning what the yarn is made of.

When making a granny square afghan, for example, you want each piece to have the correct shape. If you've worked in a stockinette stitch, the edges tend to curl and blocking is necessary. Each piece must be pinned down and pressed. The iron setting depends on the yarn. Use a cool iron on synthetic material, but natural fibers can be pressed with a warm iron. Some blocking is done by placing a damp cloth over the shaped and pinned piece. Wait until the piece is dry before removing the pins. It is not advisable to press over a garter stitch (all knit).

Assembling pieces

There are many ways to assemble the pieces of a project that must be stitched together. Some patterns here recommend leaving enough of a tail of the yarn being used to sew pieces together. In this way you have the yarn in place for the pieces and everything matches.

Main seams are usually joined with a backstitch. Use a blunt yarn needle, and with right sides of fabric together, make small stitches across the material just below the finished edges.

To join sections of ribbing, use an overcast stitch. With right sides together and edges matching, overcast the yarn on both pieces. Do not pull the yarn too taut. Keep yarn loose for a flat seam.

Another way to join seams, especially for bulky yarn, is with a slip stitch crochet. (See crochet how-to's on page 112.)

Knitting abbreviations

beg—beginning
CC—contrasting color
CL—cable left
CR—cable right
dec—decrease
dp—double-pointed needles
inc—increase
k—knit
LH—left-hand needle
lp—loop
MC—main color
p—purl
pat—pattern
psso—pass slip stitch over
rem—remaining
rep—repeat
RH—right-hand needle
rnd—round
sk—skip
sl—slip
sl st—slip stitch
st—stitch
sts—stitches
tog—together
wyib—with yarn in back
wyif—with yarn in front
yo—yarn over needle
*—repeat what comes after

Embroidery stitches

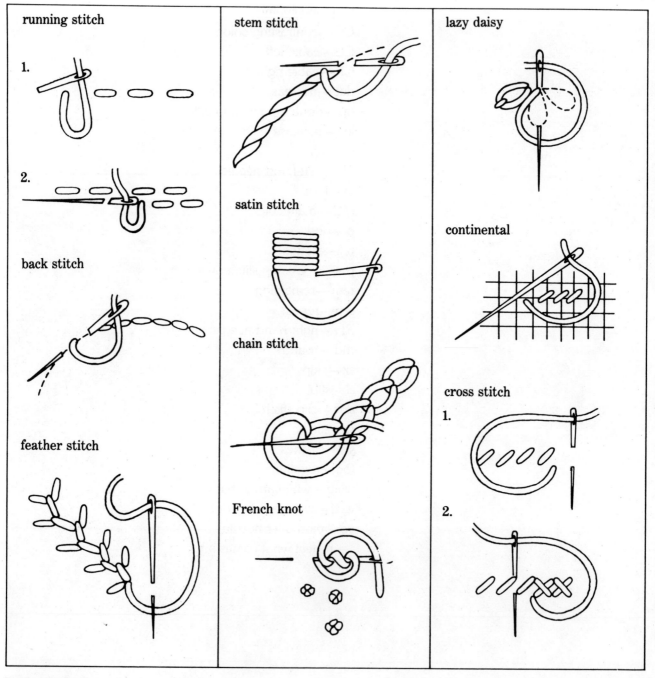

running stitch

1.

2.

back stitch

feather stitch

stem stitch

satin stitch

chain stitch

French knot

lazy daisy

continental

cross stitch

1.

2.

Basic stitches

Checkerboard afghan

The red, white, and blue afghan is easy and fun to make. Best of all, it is portable, because each square is made separately. It is then sewn together with a border of 4 strips. There is a feeling of accomplishment as you finish each square.

The design is a classic one and can be worked in a variety of colors. However, the combination of berry, indigo blue, and oatmeal is a nice variation on the traditional red, white, and blue theme and has both an American and a French country feeling.

The finished project measures 40×58 inches. Each square is 6×6 inches. To enlarge the design, simply add more rows of individual squares in keeping with the design, and be sure to add 6 inches to each short border piece for every added row of squares, and to each long border piece for every added tier.

Materials: Bucilla St. Moritz bulky weight—5 skeins oatmeal, 3 skeins berry, 6 skeins blue.
Needles: #10
Gauge: 7 sts = 2 inches
        10 rows = 2 inches

Directions

Pattern: For each square, cast on 20 sts in main color.
All stockinette st (k 1 row, p 1 row).
Work 8 rows in main color (MC).
Work 2 rows in contrasting color (CC).
Work 8 more rows in MC.
Work 2 rows in CC again.
Work 8 more rows in MC (28 rows total).
Bind off loosely.

Follow the pattern and make the following:
14 squares in blue with white stripes
13 squares in red with white stripes
14 squares in white with red stripes
13 squares in white with blue stripes

Border: Using blue yarn, cast on 12 sts.
Work entire piece in stockinette st for 54 inches.

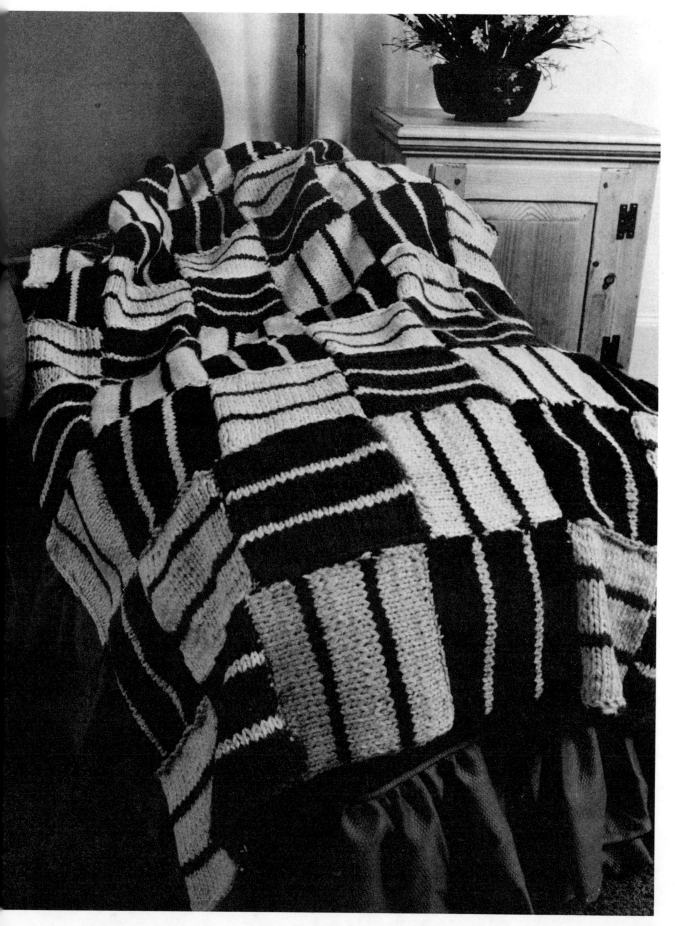

Make 2. Bind off loosely.

Using blue yarn, cast on 12 sts.

Work entire piece in stockinette st for 44 inches.

Make 2. Bind off loosely.

Blocking: Blocking is especially important with a project done in stockinette stitch, because the edges curl under. Blocking will ensure the shape desired.

Draw a 6×6-inch rectangle on paper and pin to ironing board or flat padded surface. Place each square wrong side up. Use pins along edges of square to keep it in shape within the paper square, and check measurements as you do so. Finished square should be 6×6 inches. Do not pull knitted piece out of shape as you work.

Place a dry cloth over the square and press with a cool iron. This is a synthetic yarn; however, if you are using a natural-fiber yarn, press with a slightly damp cloth and warm iron. Remove pins and continue to block each square in this way.

Block border strips in the same way, doing a few inches at a time until you have blocked the entire strip.

Finish: Follow diagram for putting finished squares together. With right sides together, sew bottom edges of 2 squares together. Open so that one is above the other. (Be sure that stripes are going in correct direction according to diagram.) Continue to sew squares in vertical rows.

Place first row of squares faceup. Place 2nd row facedown on the first row, lining up squares so seams match.

Stitch inside edge and open flat. Continue to sew each successive row of squares to the rest in this manner.

With all squares attached and faceup, place one side-border strip facedown on first row of squares with edges matching. Stitch together. Open flat. Repeat on opposite side. Do the same on top and bottom of afghan with the short border strips.

A—*Blue with white stripes*
B—*Red with white stripes*
C—*White with red stripes*
D—*White with blue stripes*

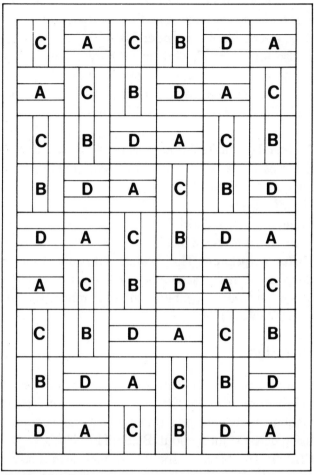

Assembly diagram

Paintbox coverlet

You'll find this a perfect baby gift. The acrylic yarn is completely washable, and the total cost for this carriage or crib blanket is under $10.

Use your leftover yarn in primary colors for the paintbox stripes, or you can purchase 1-2-3 ply Persian-type yarn that comes in 12-yard skeins. The finished afghan measures 30×37 inches.

Materials: Bucilla Wonderknit acrylic 3-oz. skeins—5 skeins white, small amount of red, green, yellow, blue, and orange.

Needles: #9

Gauge: 9 sts = 2 inches
        13 rows = 2 inches

Color sequence: The 6 white strips are 6 inches deep or 27 rows, separated by 2 rows of red (A), green (B), yellow (C), blue (D), and orange (E). End with 27 rows of white.

Directions

Cast on 136 sts with white yarn. Work in garter stitch (all knit) for 27 rows. Change to color A for 2 rows. Change to white and continue in color sequence using garter st throughout. Bind off loosely.

Finish: The blocking should be done with a steam iron and a light hand. Run iron over the back of the afghan. Lift and press as you go over each section. Be careful to keep the iron from flattening the stitches.

Painted desert

The interest in this afghan lies in the use of color. The bold stripes of yellow, red, black, and white make a definite statement, but there is nothing complicated about the project. Worked in stockinette stitch, there are 3 panels, each 22 × 48, which are joined. The finished afghan is 48 × 66 inches.

Materials: Bucilla Softex orlon 3-oz. skeins (interchangeable with knitting worsted)—6 skeins Crimson (red), 6 skeins Sun Gold, 4 skeins black, and 3 skeins white.

Needles: #8

Gauge: 9 sts = 2 inches
          7 rows = 1 inch

Color code: Black A
          Yellow B
          Red C
          White D

Directions

Cast on 99 sts in A.
Rows 1 and 2: All knit
Row 3: Knit
Row 4: Purl
Continue stockinette st (1 row k, 1 row p) for a total of 7 rows in A.
Work 7 rows B stockinette st. Change to C.

This example of the Painted desert is made from t panels. See diagram p. 37 for the three-panel version.

Work in stockinette st for 14 rows. Change to B and work 7 rows. Change to D and work 7 rows.

Continue in stockinette st in color sequence as follows:

7 rows B
7 rows D
7 rows B
14 rows A
21 rows C
7 rows A
7 rows C
7 rows B
7 rows C
7 rows D
7 rows C
7 rows D
7 rows B
7 rows D
7 rows C
7 rows D
7 rows A
7 rows D
21 rows B
7 rows A
7 rows B
7 rows C
7 rows A
20 rows C
8 rows A
7 rows C
5 rows A
14 rows B
7 rows C
14 rows D
14 rows B

5 rows A in stockinette st, then work last 2 rows of A all knit (garter st). Bind off.

Make 3 panels of this color sequence.

Finish: Carefully match each panel in color sequence as indicated in diagram. Stitch together (see page 24).

To block, steam press lightly from wrong side.

To make fringed edges, see page 92.

a b c b d b d b a   c   a c b c d c d b d c d a d   b   a b c a   c   a c a b c d   b a

Assembly diagram

White on white

The elegance of this afghan is a result of the material and stitches as well as color restraint. Designed by Bee Gonella, this lovely lap throw is made with a silk wool blend that makes it extremely soft. The material handles more like cotton than wool.

Made in 3 strips for ease of handling, it incorporates many traditional fisherman's patterns, alternating the horizontal with the vertical. The finished project is 49 × 60 inches.

Materials: Tahki Chelsea silk 100-gram balls—11 skeins Ecru.
Needles: #8, #29 circular needles
Gauge: 4 sts = 1 inch
       6 rows = 1 inch

Directions

Pattern A: The following pattern includes stockinette st, mock cable, twisted diamond, plain cable, tree of life, small horseshoe cable.
Row 1: K 3, p 1, k 3, p 1, k 1, p 4, k 2, p 4, k 4, p 2, k 4, p 2, k 3, p 4, k 3, p 4, k 3, p 1, k 4, p 1, k 3.
Row 2: Knit all k sts and purl all p sts.
Row 3: K 3, p 1, k 3, p 1, k 4, *p 3, CR, p 2, CL, p 3,* k 4, p 2, k 4, p 2, k 3, *p 3, CR, k 1, CL, p 3,* k 3, p 1, k 1, p 1, k 3.
Row 4: Purl all purl sts and knit all k sts.
Row 5: K 3, p 1, slip 2, k 1, pass 1st st over the 2nd st, p 1, k 4, p 2, CR, p 4, CL, p 2, k 4, p 2, k 4, p 2, k 3, p 2, CR, p 1, k 1, p 1, CL, k 2, k 3, p 1, CR, CL, p 1, k 3.
Row 6: Knit all k sts, purl all p sts until you get to last 6 sts. K 1, p 1, yo, p 1, k 1, p 3.
Row 7: K 3, p 1, k 3, p 1, k 4, p 1, CR, p 6, CL, p 1, k 4, p 2, cable 2 st, k 2, p 2, k 3, p 1, CR, p 1, k 3, p 1, CL, p 1, k 3, p 1, k 4, p 1, k 3.
Row 8: Same as row 2.
Row 9: K 3, p 1, sl 2, k 1, pass first slip st over 2, p 1, k 4, p 1, CL, p 4, CR, p 1, k 4, p 2, k 4, p 2, k 3, p 3, CR, k 1, CL, p 3, k 3, p 1, CR, CL, p 1, k 3.
Row 10: Same as row 6.
Row 11: K 3, p 1, k 3, p 1, k 4, p 2, CL, p 2, CR, p 2,

The elegance of this afghan is a result of the material and stitches as well as color restraint. Designed by Bee Gonella, this lovely lap throw is made with a silk wool blend that makes it extremely soft. The material handles more like cotton than wool.

Made in 3 strips for ease of handling, it incorporates many traditional fisherman's patterns, alternating the horizontal with the vertical. The finished project is 49×60 inches.

Materials: Tahki Chelsea silk 100-gram balls—11 skeins Ecru.
Needles: #8, #29 circular needles
Gauge: 4 sts = 1 inch
$\qquad$ 6 rows = 1 inch

Directions

Pattern A: The following pattern includes stockinette st, mock cable, twisted diamond, plain cable, tree of life, small horseshoe cable.

Row 1: K 3, p 1, k 3, p 1, k 1, p 4, k 2, p 4, k 4, p 2, k 4, p 2, k 3, p 4, k 3, p 4, k 3, p 1, k 4, p 1, k 3.

Row 2: Knit all k sts and purl all p sts.

Row 3: K 3, p 1, k 3, p 1, k 4, *p 3, CR, p 2, CL, p 3,* k 4, p 2, k 4, p 2, k 3, *p 3, CR, k 1, CL, p 3,* k 3, p 1, k 1, p 1, k 3.

Row 4: Purl all purl sts and knit all k sts.

Row 5: K 3, p 1, slip 2, k 1, pass 1st st over the 2nd st, p 1, k 4, p 2, CR, p 4, CL, p 2, k 4, p 2, k 4, p 2, k 3, p 2, CR, p 1, k 1, p 1, CL, k 2, k 3, p 1, CR, CL, p 1, k 3.

Row 6: Knit all k sts, purl all p sts until you get to last 6 sts. K 1, p 1, yo, p 1, k 1, p 3.

Row 7: K 3, p 1, k 3, p 1, k 4, p 1, CR, p 6, CL, p 1, k 4, p 2, cable 2 st, k 2, p 2, k 3, p 1, CR, p 1, k 3, p 1, CL, p 1, k 3, p 1, k 4, p 1, k 3.

Row 8: Same as row 2.

Row 9: K 3, p 1, sl 2, k 1, pass first slip st over 2, p 1, k 4, p 1, CL, p 4, CR, p 1, k 4, p 2, k 4, p 2, k 3, p 3, CR, k 1, CL, p 3, k 3, p 1, CR, CL, p 1, k 3.

Row 10: Same as row 6.

Row 11: K 3, p 1, k 3, p 1, k 4, p 2, CL, p 2, CR, p 2, k 4, p 2, k 4, p 2, k 3, p 2, CR, p 1, k 1, p 1, CL, p 2, k 3, p 1, k 4, p 1, k 3.

Row 12: Same as row 2.

Row 13: K 3, p 1, sl 2 k 1, psso 2, p 1, k 4, p 3, CL, CR, p 3, k 4, p 2, cable 2 stockinette st, k 2, p 2, k 3, p 1, CR, p 1, k 3, p 1, CL, p 1, k 3, p 1, CR, CL, p 1, k 3.

Row 14: Same as row 6.

Row 15: K 3, p 1, k 3, p 1, k 4, p 4, CR, p 4, k 4, p 2, k 4, p 2, k 3, p 3, CR, k 1, CL, p 3, k 3, p 1, k 4, p 1, k 3.

Row 16: Same as row 2.

Row 17: K 3, p 1, sl 2, k 1, psso 2, p 1, k 4, p 3, CR, CL, p 3, k 4, p 2, k 4, p 2, k 3, p 2, CR, p 1, k 1, p 1, CL, p 2, k 3, p 1, CR, CL, p 1, k 3.

Row 18: Same as row 6.

Continue in this pattern until 7 diamonds have been completed (108 rows).

Work 8 rows of seed st (k 1, p 1, k 1 across, row 2: p 1, k 1, p 1 across).

Pattern B: Work 8 rows of seed st. Then, beginning with a knit row, do 4 rows of stockinette st.

The next 12 rows are parallelogram check.

Row 1: * K 5, p 5, rep from * across.

Row 2: K 4, * p 5, k 5, rep from * ending p 5, k 1.

Row 3: P 2 *, k 5, p 5, rep from * ending k 5, p 3.

Row 4: K 2, * p 5, k 5, rep from * ending p 5, k 3.

Row 5: P 4, * k 5, p 5, rep from * ending k 5, p 1.

Row 6: P 5, k 5*, rep from * across.

Repeat rows 1 through 6.

Work next 4 rows in stockinette st.

Row 13: Knit

Row 14: Purl

Rows 15 through 20: Knit

Repeat rows 13 through 20.

Work 4 rows in stockinette st.

Next 2 rows knit

2 rows stockinette st

12 rows double-diamond brocade as follows:

Row 1: K 5, * p 2, k 10, rep from * end with p 2, k 5.

Row 2 and all even rows: Knit all k sts and purl all p sts.

Row 3: K 3, * p 2, k 2, p 2, k 6, rep from * ending k 3.

Row 5: K 1, * p 2, k 6, p 2, k 2, rep from * ending k 1.

Row 7: P 1, * k 10, p 2, rep from * ending k 10, p 1.

Row 9: Same as row 5.

Row 11: Same as row 3.

Row 12: Same as row 2.

Work 2 rows all knit.

4 rows stockinette st

5 rows open work as follows:

Row 1: Purl

Row 2: K 1, * yo, k 2 tog, rep from * across.

Row 3: Same as row 2.

Row 4: All knit

Rows 5 through 8: Stockinette st

12 rows basket weave as follows:

Row 1: Knit

Row 2: K 2, * p 2, k 4, rep from * ending k 2.

Row 3: P 2, * k 2, p 4, rep from * ending p 2.

Row 4: Same as row 2.

Repeat these 4 rows 3 times.

Work next 4 rows in stockinette st.

Next 8 rows coral knot st as follows:

Row 1: K 1, * k 2 tog, rep from * ending k 1.

Row 2: K 1, * k 1 insert needle under running thread of st just worked and knit this thread. Rep from * ending k 1.

Row 3: Knit

Row 4: Purl

Repeat rows 1 through 4.

Work next 2 rows in stockinette st.

Next 2 rows knit

2 rows purl

2 rows stockinette st

8 rows seed st (k 1, p 1 on first row, p 1, k 1 on next row)

Repeat Pattern A, omitting the last 8 rows of seed st.

Assembly diagram

Panel 1

Cast on 68 sts.

Work first 3 sts, k 1, p 1, k 1. Follow Pattern B, ending with k 1, p 1, k 1, p 1, k 1 for the last 5 sts.

This will give you a seed st border. Next work Pattern A, then another B.

Panel 2

Cast on 60 sts.

Work Pattern A, then B, then another A, omitting last 8 rows seed st (k 1, p 1).

Panel 3

Cast on 68 sts.

Work first 5 sts k 1, p 1, k 1, p 1, k 1 and last 3 sts, k 1, p 1, k 1. Follow Patterns B, A, B.

Finish: Follow diagram and assemble panels 1, 2, and 3 with a running backstitch. After they are joined, use your circular needle to pick up 194 sts and work in seed st for 9 rows at both the bottom and top edges to finish.

Cloudspun

To achieve this light, airy cloudspun look, use a mohair blend yarn on a needle size a bit larger than usually recommended for this type of yarn. Here the afghan is soft and fluffy and the yardage from this yarn is quite good at 174 yards per 50-gram skein. You can substitute a sport or worsted if you prefer.

The finished coverlet is 42×56 inches plus the fringed edges, and the entire piece is all knit (garter stitch).

Materials: Phildar Dedicace 50-gram skeins—4 skeins each of wine and deep rose, 3 skeins each of pale pink and soft green.
Needles: #11
Gauge: 4 sts = 1 inch
      6 rows = 1¼ inches

Color code: Wine A
          Deep rose B
          Pale pink C
          Soft green D

Directions

Each band of color is 2½ inches deep. There are 6 bands each of A, B, C, and D.

Begin with A and cast on 168 sts. Knit across. Continue for 12 rows or 2½ inches in this color. Change to B on right side and knit for 2½ inches. Continue, following color pattern.

Fringe: Cut 6 strands of each color 12 inches long for each fringe. Fold in half. Use a crochet hook to draw folded end through space in stitches from right to wrong side. Pull the loose fringe ends through the folded strands and draw a tight knot.

Keeping the color sequence, space fringe approximately 1 inch apart. Trim ends of fringe so they are even.

Country hearts

Everyone loves hearts, and this afghan is a wonderful example of how you can use color as well as stitches in a design. The charts will help you place the stitches. Some panels are worked with raspberry-colored yarn, while others duplicate the pattern in white on white.

Composed of 6-inch squares, the finished afghan measures 54 × 78 inches. There are 13 rows of 9 Squares each.

Materials: Settlement Farm 2-ply worsted wool (see Source list for ordering yarn)—10 skeins raspberry, 15 skeins natural.
Needles: #8
Gauge: 9 sts = 2 inches
13 rows = 2 inches

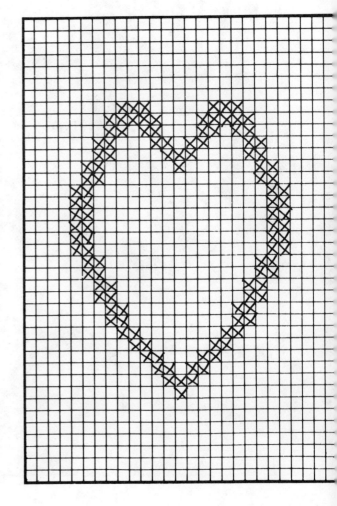

Directions

Make 82 plain white squares.
Cast on 27 sts.
Rows 1 and 2: K 1, p 1 across.
Rows 3 through 37: Stockinette st (knit 1 row, purl 1 row).
Rows 38 and 39: K 1, p 1 across.
Make 18 white squares with pink hearts.
Cast on 27 sts.
Rows 1 and 2: K 1, p 1, across.
Rows 3, 5, and 7: Purl
Rows 4 and 6: Knit
Rows 8 through 32: Refer to diagram for stitch placement.
Rows 33, 35, and 37: Purl
Rows 34 and 36: Knit
Rows 38 and 39: K 1, p 1 across.
Make 17 pink squares with heart design.
With pink, cast on 27 sts and follow pattern for preceding hearts. Follow Charts 1 and 2 and purl all squares shown with an X.

B	A	C	A	B	A	C	A	B
A	A	A	A	A	A	A	A	A
C	A	B	A	C	A	B	A	C
A	A	A	A	A	A	A	A	A
B	A	C	A	B	A	C	A	B
A	A	A	A	A	A	A	A	A
C	A	B	A	C	A	B	A	C
A	A	A	A	A	A	A	A	A
B	A	C	A	B	A	C	A	B
A	A	A	A	A	A	A	A	A
C	A	B	A	C	A	B	A	C

Assembly diagram

A—Plain white
B—White with pink heart
C—Pink with heart

Finish: Follow diagram and stitch all squares together.

Edging: Work 1 row double crochet (dc) around edge. Work 2 rows dc in white. Work 1 row dc in pink. Fasten off.

See page 24 for blocking.

Embroidery for baby

When a new baby is on the way, this delicately embroidered coverlet is the perfect welcoming gift. It can be made in any of the soft baby colors with matching or contrasting floral colors.

The texture of garter stitch and stockinette stitch adds interest, and the panels create a checkerboard effect with the embroidery in the solid areas. Made entirely of one color background, there is no changing of yarn as you go along. The designs are added after the afghan is complete This project can be knit with knitting worsted, wool, or washable acrylic (shown here).

Materials: Bernat "Berella 4" acrylic 4-ply yarn 3½-oz. skeins—4 skeins pale yellow, small amounts of green, orange, and white (1-2-3 ply Persian-type yarn comes in 12-yard skeins and all colors); Trace-Erase (optional). TraceErase is a gauzelike backing paper that is sold in fabric shops for the purpose of doing appliqué or embroidery. It will help in the placement of your designs.

Needles: #8

Gauge: 8 sts = 2 inches
        13 rows = 2 inches

Directions

The finished blanket is 32 × 40 inches. It is made in one piece with 8 rows of 8 panels each. Each panel is 4 × 5 inches. With yellow, cast on 128 sts.

Row 1: *K 16, p 16. Repeat from * across.

Row 2: Purl across.

Row 3: Repeat row 1.

Row 4 and all even rows through row 32: Purl across.

Row 5 and all odd rows through row 31: *K 16, p 16. Repeat from * across.

Row 33: *P 16, k 16, rep from * across.

Row 34 and all even rows through 64: Purl across.

Row 35 and all odd rows through 63: *P 16, k 16. Repeat from * across.

Continue this pattern to end. There will be 64 panels (32 stockinette, 32 garter stitch).

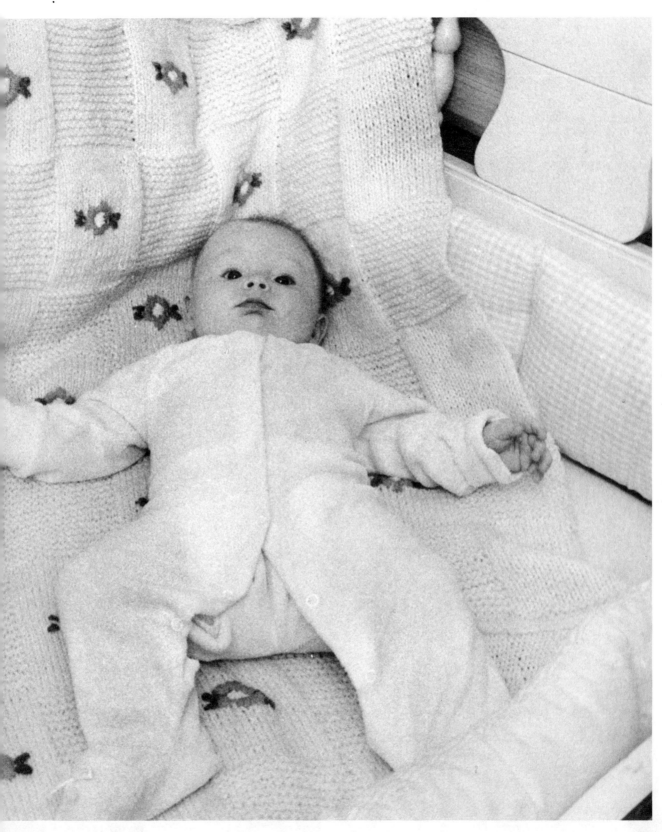

Embroidery: The easiest way to transfer the floral design to the afghan is with TraceErase. This is a special loosely woven paper that prevents stitches from puckering and slipping and will allow you to embroider easily. When finished, you can tear away the paper for perfect results.

Trace the flowers as many times as needed. Cut out a square with space around the flower and pin in place on the background. Use the stitch guide on page 26 to embroider each flower. Do not make knots on the underside of your work. If you leave a 2-inch tail at the beginning and end of each new thread, you can weave these ends into the yarn when finished.

Finish: Pad ironing board. Place afghan facedown and steam press. Block to size.

embroidered square

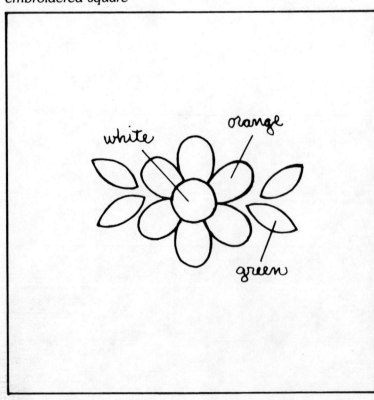

Navaho afghan

Based on an Indian rug design, this afghan has a strong pattern in black and red. The yarn used is an elegantly classic sport weight that feels and looks refined.

Although at first glance this design may look complicated, it is not difficult as it is made in 4 separate strips using the stockinette st. It can, of course, also be made in one unit. The argyle method of 2-color knitting is employed and it is worked from bottom to top. Finished size is 48 × 68 inches.

Each panel is 12 × 68 inches.

Materials: Phildar Schema sportyarn 50-gram balls —8 skeins each of Noir (black) and Pavot (red), red and black bobbins
Needles: #10
Gauge: 4 sts = 1 inch
6 rows = 1 inch

54

Directions

The work is done with 2 strands plyed together. With red, cast on 48 sts. Knit across 2 rows.

If done on round needles, cast on 196 sts.

Pattern 1: Stockinette st (k 1 row, p 1 row)

6 inches in red

6 rows (1 inch) black

6 rows red

5 inches black

5 rows red

1 row black

5 rows red

1 row black

5 rows red

Pattern 2

2 inches black (knit)

6 rows stockinette st 28 sts in red, * 16 black, 4 red (tie in red bobbin) (for rnd needles, 32 red, rep from *, ending in 4 red)

Work next 6 rows 4 red (tie in black bobbin), * 20 black sts, 4 red, 12 black, 12 red (for rnd needles, rep from *)

Work next 6 rows 4 sts red, * 4 black, 20 red, 8 black, and 16 red (for rnd needles, rep from *).

Work next 6 rows 4 sts red, * 28 black, 20 red (rep from *).

Work next 4 inches all red.

1 row black

5 rows red

1 row black

5 rows red

1 row black

5 rows red

Repeat Pattern 2 three more times.

Pattern 3

Work 5 inches in black.

Work 1 inch in red.

1 inch black

6 inches red, ending with 2 rows garter st.

Bind off on the knit side to finish.

Make 4 of these strips following the patterns.

Match all colors and stitches and carefully join each

Navaho afghan

panel with a running backstitch. (See page 92 for fringe.)

Woven rug pattern

Inspired by a woven rug, this blue and white pattern is knit with Bernat's Sesame "4," a traditional 4-ply knitting worsted weight yarn. It is warm, wrinkle-resistant, and moisture resistant; the colors are rich yet subtle. This yarn is interchangeable with any knitting worsted that meets the gauge requirements. Finished afghan is 48 × 66 inches.

Materials: Knitting worsted 4-oz. skeins—5 skeins white, 7 skeins blue, 5 large bobbins
Needles: #10
Gauge: 4 sts = 1 inch
      6 rows = 1 inch

Directions

The afghan is made in pieces. There are 4 corner sections, 2 borders with short stripes, 2 border sections with long stripes (on sides). The center is made as another piece. When finished, the afghan is pieced together to create the whole. The stockinette st is used for the outside pieces with a flat diamond pattern for the center piece. The argyle method of changing colors is used on the outside pieces. When finished, all parts are stitched together.
Pattern 1: Make 4.
Begin each knit row of 2 of these panels with a seed st of k 1, p 1, k 1 for 3 sts only. End each purl row with k 1, p 1, k 1. This keeps the edges from curling. Reverse this for the other 2 panels.
Cast on 48 sts in the following way:
8 blue, 8 white, 16 blue, 8 white, 8 blue. Tie ends together.
Rows 1 through 12: Work 8 sts blue, 8 white, 16 blue, 8 white, and 8 blue.
Rows 13 through 24: Work 8 white, 8 blue, 16 white, 8 blue, 8 white.
Rows 25 through 48: Work 8 blue, 8 white, 16 blue, 8 white, 8 blue.
Rows 49 through 60: Work 8 white, 8 blue, 16 white, 8 blue, 8 white.
Rows 61 through 72: Work 8 blue, 8 white, 16 blue, 8 white, and 8 blue.
Pattern 2: Make 2.

With white, cast on 95 sts.

Work 12 rows in stockinette st all white.

Work next 12 rows (2 inches) all blue.

Next 4 inches white

Next 2 inches blue

Last 2 inches (72 rows in all) white. Bind off loosely.

Pattern 3: Make 1.

This can be made entirely in stockinette st for 42 inches, or you can use the following pattern for a textured piece.

Cast on 95 sts blue.

Row 1: K 3, * p 1, k 7, rep from * ending p 1, k 3.

Row 2: P 2, * k 1, p 1, k 1, p 5, rep from * ending k 1, p 1, k 1, p 2.

Row 3: K 1, * p 1, k 3, rep from * ending p 1, k 1.

Row 4: K 1, * p 5, k 1, p 1, k 1, rep from * ending p 5, k 1.

Row 5: * K 7, p 1, rep from * ending k 7.

Row 6: Same as row 4.

Row 7: Same as row 3.

Row 8: Same as row 2.

Repeat these 8 rows until piece measures 42 inches.

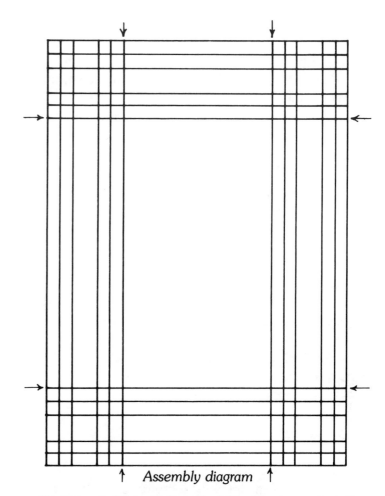

Assembly diagram

Pattern 4: Make 2 (1 with right edge in seed st, 1 with left edge in seed st—k 1, p 1, k 1).

Cast on 48 sts as follows:

8 white, 8 blue, 16 white, 8 blue, 8 white. Tie connecting ends together. Work in stockinette st, maintaining the seed border on either the right or left side. Work for 42 inches. Bind off loosely.

Assembly: Sew 1 square Pattern 1 with seed border on left side to 1 piece of Pattern 2. Sew another square to right side of Pattern 1 (see diagram).

Repeat with remaining pieces of Patterns 1 and 2. Attach side borders (Pattern 4) to center panel (Pattern 3) making sure that seed borders are on right and left edges.

Join all pieces with horizontal seams (see diagram for final piecing).

Finish: Block and steam press from wrong side (see page 24). You might want to add fringes at both ends. If so, refer to page 92 for directions.

Nature's stripes

The warm harmony of nature's shades is used to create this classic pattern. Curl up by a fireplace with the added cozy comfort of this all-wool afghan that will last for years and years.

Work the chevron pattern from bottom to top for a finished size of 48 × 66 inches. Seven colors are used here, but you can create any color scheme you want. This is the perfect project to design for your environment. Just use the stitch pattern with the colors of your choice. For a dramatic, bold effect, try white with another color such as red or navy blue, alternating every 3 inches.

Materials: Bernat Sesame wool worsted weight 3-oz. skeins—4 skeins each of luggage, beige, pale olive, Ranchero red, moss green, cinnamon, and terra cotta.

Needles: #8

Gauge: 5 sts = 1 inch
       7 rows = 1 inch

Color code: Terra cotta A
          Green B
          Red C
          Cinnamon (light brown) D
          Pale olive E
          Beige F
          Luggage (brown) G

Directions

With A, cast on 82 sts. Work the 22 rows of the stitch pattern as follows:

Stitch pattern: Chevron stripe of 1 color = 3 inches plus 1 row.

Row 1: K 1, * k 9, p 2, k 9, rep from * ending k 1.

Row 2: P 1, * p 8, k 4, p 8, rep from * ending p 1.

Row 3: K 1, * k 7, p 2, k 2, p 2, k 7, rep from * ending k 1.

Row 4: P 1, * p 6, k 2, p 4, k 2, p 6, rep from * ending p 1.

Row 5: K 1, * k 5, p 2, k 6, p 2, k 5, rep from * ending k 1.

Row 6: P 1, * p 4, k 2, p 8, k 2, p 4, rep from *

ending p 1.

Row 7: K 1, * k 3, p 2, k 10, p 2, k 3, rep from * ending k 1.

Row 8: P 1, * p 2, k 2, p 12, k 2, p 2, rep from * ending p 1.

Row 9: K 1, * k 1, p 2, k 14, p 2, k 2, rep from * ending k 1.

Row 10: P 1, * k 2, p 16, k 2, rep from * ending p 1.

Row 11: K 1, * p 1, k 18, p 1, rep from * ending k 1.

Row 12: P 1, * p 9, k 2, p 9, rep from * ending p 1.

Row 13: K 1, * k 8, p 4, k 8, rep from * ending k 1.

Row 14: P 1, * p 7, k 2, p 2, k 2, p 7, rep from * ending p 1.

Row 15: K 1, * k 6, p 2, k 4, p 2, k 6, rep from * ending k 1.

Row 16: P 1, * p 5, k 2, p 6, k 2, p 5, rep from * ending p 1.

Row 17: K 1, * k 4, p 2, k 8, p 2, k 4, rep from * ending k 1.

Row 18: P 1, * p 3, k 2, p 10, k 2, p 3, rep from * ending p 1.

Row 19: K 1, * k 2, p 2, k 12, p 2, k 2, rep from * ending k 1.

Row 20: P 1, * p 1, k 2, p 14, k 2, p 1, rep from * ending p 1.

Row 21: K 1, * p 2, k 16, p 2, rep from * ending k 1.

Row 22: P 1, * k 1, p 18, k 1, rep from * ending p 1.

Work stitch pattern in the following color sequence:

A—B—C—D—E—F—A—B—G—C—D—E—
F—A—G—C—D—E—F—A—B

Each stripe is one complete pattern of 22 rows.

This project can be made in 3 separate pieces for ease when carrying your work with you. If made this way, you will work from bottom to top, making 3 pieces of the color sequence in the stitch pattern.

When working the left and right panels, keep the first st and the last st in garter st (knit). This will keep the edges of the afghan from curling.

Finish: With stitches aligned and yarn colors matching, join sections with a running backstitch. Add fringe if desired (see page 92).

B
A
F
E
D
C
G
A
F
E
D
C
G
B
A
F
E
D
C
B
A

Assembly diagram

All-American

Made in squares and then stitched together, this afghan can be carried with you for odd moments of crafting. The material is a bulky yarn worked on large needles, which will make it quick and fun to do. The red, white, and blue color scheme is more subtle than you'll find in some of the other projects with the same color combination.

The waffle stitch gives a nice texture and makes the blanket extremely warm. The pattern stitch is easy to do and even a beginning knitter will find this do-able.

The squares are 9 inches and the finished afghan is 54 × 72 inches.

Materials: Tahki Bulky Donegal 3½-oz. skeins—10 skeins each color: red #344, blue #343, and white #338.

Needles: #10½

Gauge: 5½ sts = 2 inches

  13 rows = 2 inches

Directions

Make 48. Cast on 25 sts in red.

Work 1 row knit as a setup row.

Work 5 repeats of pattern in red.

Work 5 repeats of pattern in white.

Work 5 repeats of pattern in blue.

Bind off loosely.

Pattern: Waffle fabric stitch

Row 1: Knit all sts.

Row 2: * K 1, k the st under the next st, removing both sts from LH needle as one, rep from *, end k 1.

Row 3: Knit all sts.

Row 4: * K the st under the first st as above, k 1, rep from * ending k under. Bind off loosely.

Assembly diagram

Baby starbursts

Knit rows of star patterns for your favorite baby. Here the color combination is mint green, peach, and white. You can also make this with leftover, pastel yarns so that every other row is a different color divided by a row of white. Or, make it in all white for a beautiful christening robe.

This afghan is 27×32 inches and is a perfect size for wrapping up that newborn baby when leaving the hospital.

Materials: Bucilla Softex washable acrylic 4-oz. skeins—1 skein pale sage (A), 1 skein peach (B), 2 skeins white.

Needles: #8 and #13 needles, 14 inches long; #8 circular needle, 29 inches; #13 circular needle, 36 inches; 8 markers.

Crochet hook: F

Gauge: 9 sts = 2 inches
         5 rows = 1 inch

Directions

With white MC cast on 121 sts to #8 needles.

Row 1: With #13 needle (right side), knit.

Row 2: With #8 needle, * p 3 tog, do not slip sts off LH needle, yo, p same 3 sts tog, sl sts off LH needle, k 1, rep from * across, end last repeat k 1, p 1.

Row 3: Change to green A and knit with #8 needles.

Row 4: With #13 needles, p 1, * k 1, p 3 tog, do not slip sts off LH needle, yo, p same 3 sts tog, sl sts off left needle, repeat from * across.

Repeat rows 1 and 2 with MC and rows 3 and 4 with peach B. Go back to MC for rows 1 and 2 again and continue this pattern to end (16 groups of 4—white, green, white, peach).

The border is optional, but adds a finishing touch.

Border: With green and #8 circular needle, k across 121 sts on needle. Put a marker on needle.

Pick up and k 1 st in corner. Place a marker on needle.

Pick up and k 101 sts evenly spaced on side edge. Put a marker on the needle.

Pick up and k 1 st in corner. Put a marker on needle.

Pick up and k 121 sts on cast-on edge. Put a marker on needle.

Pick up and k 1 st in corner. Put a marker on needle. Pick up and k 101 sts evenly spaced on side edge. Put marker on needle. Pick up and k 1 st in corner. Put marker on needle (8 markers) 448 sts.
Slipping markers, work around as follows:

Rnd 1: Knit.

Rnd 2: * K to corner st, yo, k 1 (corner st), yo, rep from * around.

Rnds 3 and 4: Repeat rnds 1 and 2 (464 sts).

Rnd 5: Knit. Drop MC and join peach B.

Rnd 6: With #13 circular needle and B, knit.

Rnd 7: With #8 circular needle and B, work pattern row 4, working k 1, yo, k 1 in each corner st. Cut B, leaving a 4-inch tail.

Rnd 8: With #8 circular needle and MC, knit. Bind off in k same tension as sts.

Edging (see pp. 108 and 112): With white MC and crochet hook from right side, work 1 rnd single crochet (sc), working 3 sc in each corner st. Join with a sl st in first sc. Do not turn.

Next rnd: * Working loosely, sl 1, ch 1, sk next st, repeat from * around. Join with sl st in first sl st. End off.

Finish: With a tapestry needle, run yarn ends under yarn on wrong side. Steam press from back, blocking to square off corners as you press.

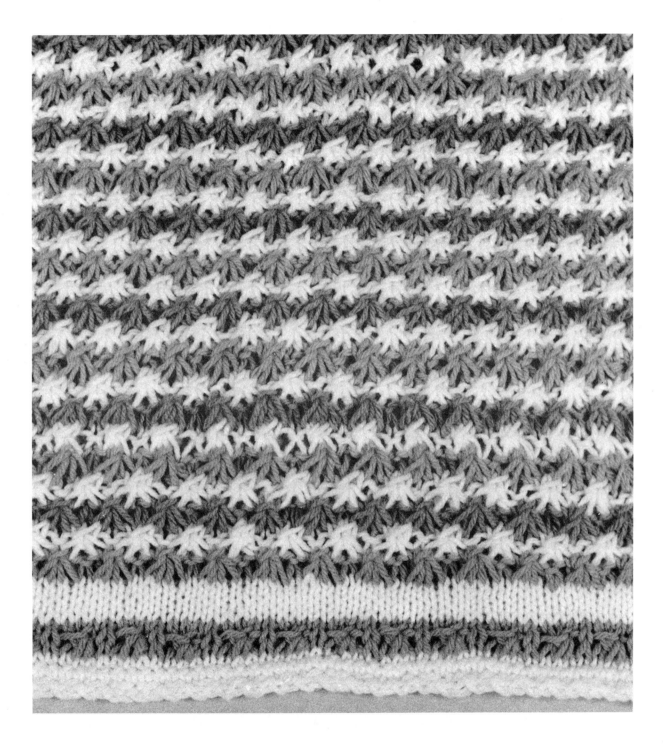

Mosaic squares

This afghan is 62 inches square and makes a nice lap throw. It is the perfect take-along project, and you'll find that each block can be made quite quickly.

Using 5 colors, you will begin with the light gray center. As the design spreads outward, the colors intensify. The surrounding blocks that make up the border are darkest aqua.

Materials: Phildar Pegase worsted weight 50-gram balls—9 skeins dark aqua #79 Prusse (A), 8 skeins #25 Cosmos aqua (B), 6 skeins #42 dark gray (C), 4 skeins #65 metal, medium gray (D), and 2 skeins #35 Flanelle light gray (E).

Needles: #10

Gauge: 5 sts = 1 inch
         7 rows = 1 inch

Directions

Each block is 4×4 inches, 4×8 inches, or 4×12 inches. You will follow the diagram for color sequence when piecing together.

Pattern: (right side)

Row 1: P 1, * k 1, p 1, rep from * across.

Row 2: K 1, * p 1, k 1, rep from * across.

Row 3: K 1, * p 1, K 1, rep from * across.

Row 4: P 1, * k 1, p 1, rep from * across.

Repeat these 4 rows for pattern.

4×4-inch square: Make 2 A, 2 B, 2 each of C and D, 3 E.

Cast on 19 sts loosely. Work in pattern for 27 rows, ending with pattern row 3. Bind off in pattern on row 23.

4×8-inch rectangle: Make 34 A, 26 B, 18 C, 10 D, and 2 E.

Cast on 39 sts. Work in pattern for same number of rows as 4×4-inch square. Bind off in pattern.

4×12-inch rectangle: Make 2 A, 2 B, 2 each of C and D, 2 E.

Cast on 59 sts. Work in pattern for same number of rows as 4×4-inch square. Bind off in pattern.

Finish: Begin at the lower edge of the diagram. On wrong side sew the bound-off edge of A square to center of large A rectangle along cast-on edge. Sew together stitch for stitch so the pattern is continuous.

Next make a strip by sewing blocks A, B, A together. Sew the first piece to this strip, centering carefully so that the outer half of each end rectangle is free. Continue to follow the diagram, always sewing the bound-off edge of the last strip to the cast-on edge of the next strip.

When finished, block entire afghan to 62 inches square.

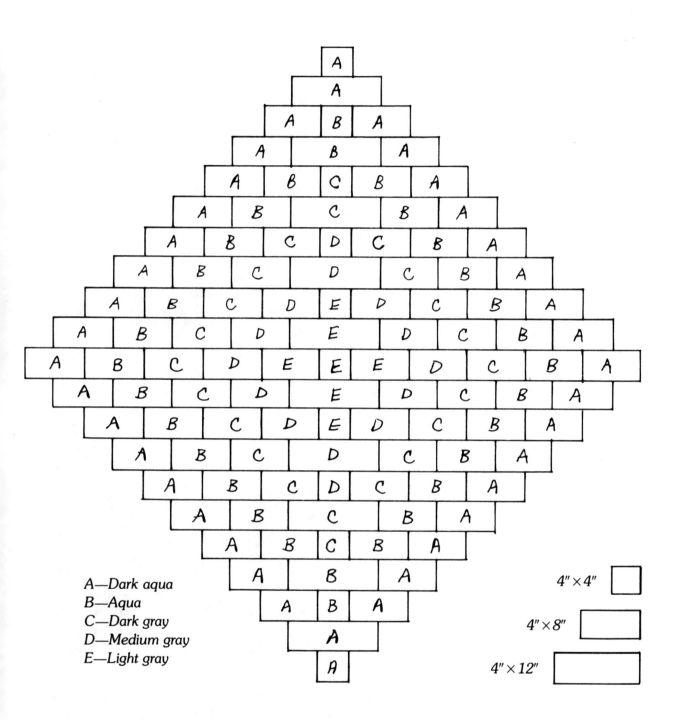

A—Dark aqua
B—Aqua
C—Dark gray
D—Medium gray
E—Light gray

4"×4"

4"×8"

4"×12"

Caribbean calypso

This is a chance to let your imagination run wild. Get out all those leftovers or have a great time choosing the brightest colors you can find. Made of 100% cotton yarn, this knit ripple design combines all the rainbow colors. It is lightweight, which makes it good for a summer throw or for those of you who live in a southern climate.

The finished afghan is 45 × 60 inches. The cotton is interchangeable with a knitting worsted for the same gauge.

Materials: Phildar Abordage cotton yarn 50-gram balls—6 balls red, 6 balls navy blue, 6 balls shocking pink, 6 balls orange, and 6 balls true blue.

Needle: #10

Gauge: Stockinette st 4 = 1 inch

Stitch pattern: Multiple of 13 sts plus 2

Directions

There are 15 bands of 5 colors repeated 3 times.

Cast on with blue 132 sts and knit one row.

Row 1: * P 2, k yo 10 times, k 1. Rep from *, end p 2.

Row 2: * K 2, p 2 tog, p 17, p 2 tog. Rep from *, end k 2.

Rows 3: * P 2, sl 1, k 1 psso, k 15, k 2 tog. Rep from *, end p 2.

Row 4: * K 2, p 2 tog, p 13, p 2 tog. Rep from *, end k 2.

Row 5: * P 2, sl 1, k 1, psso, k 11, k 2 tog. Rep from *, end p 2.

Row 6: * K 2, p 2 tog, p 9, p 2 tog. Rep from *, end k 2.

Repeat 6 rows for desired length in the following color sequence:

Blue

Orange

Pink

Navy

Red

Blue

Orange

Pink

Navy

Red

Blue

Orange

Pink

Navy

Red

Bind off sts. Weave all ends under stitches on back.

Press from back with warm iron.

Monogram afghan

A personalized bed cover makes an especially nice wedding present, or you might want to make one for yourself. This design was inspired by an Oriental rug and the natural and blue color wool is in keeping with this feeling. This is an ambitious project, but the results are well worth the time and effort.

The monograms are charted here for you so you can easily personalize your project. The finished afghan is 56 × 72 inches. Each square is 8 inches and the center panel is a 24-inch square.

Materials: Christopher Sheep Farm wool 4-oz. skeins—25 skeins white, 10 skeins blueberry, 10 skeins navy.
Needles: #8
Gauge: 5 sts = 1 inch
7 rows = 1 inch

Directions

There are 63 squares. Cast on 40 sts with white. Work each square in stockinette stitch. There are 42 squares all white. In 8 of the squares, the white is broken up with a blue design. Follow the chart for stitch placement. The corner squares have another design in the center. Follow chart for placement.

When working the 2-color squares, refer to page 22 for changing colors in the middle of the work.

To make center panel, cast on 120 sts with white. Work this panel for 168 rows or 24 inches in stockinette st. The monogram is embroidered over the background once the afghan is complete. Bind off loosely.

Blocking: It is often easiest to block each piece when making a stockinette project that is made up of many squares. In this way, you are not working with one large and heavy item, which can be cumbersome to block as one finished project.

Draw an 8-inch square on a piece of paper and pin this to your ironing board. Place each block of knitting facedown on the paper and pin at each corner. With a slightly damp cloth over the fabric, steam press lightly while working the square into the required size.

When blocking the center panel, measure the piece as you block so that you end up with a 24-inch square.

Assembly: Follow the assembly diagram when joining each panel. With right sides facing, begin with one corner panel and stitch to one white square. Continue to join squares to create the top border row, ending with another blue-and-white corner square. Repeat this on the bottom, keeping in mind that it is slightly different from the top row. First join a corner square to a white square. Next join this with the second motif blue-and-white square, joined to a white, then a motif, then a white, and end with another corner square. You now have 2 border strips for the top and bottom of your afghan.

Next join squares to make up each side border, alternating white squares with motif squares. Now you will make 4 rows of 5 white squares joined horizontally. These are the rows that will join to the center panel on the top and bottom. Join 3 white panels so that the cast-on edge of one meets the bound-off edge of the one above it. Repeat with remaining 3 squares. You now have 10 separate rows of squares.

Finish: Begin from the center out. Place 2 rows of 5 squares each (that are joined together) facedown on the top edge of the center panel. Be sure to center this so that there are 3 squares on the center panel with 1 square on either side. Sew together and open with right sides up. Repeat this on the bottom edge of the center panel.

Next, join 3 squares on each side of the center panel and stitch these side rows to the squares above and below to finish the center of the afghan. The center panel is now surrounded by 24 white squares (see diagram).

Attach outside border rows in the same way, making sure that stitches and edges match correctly.

Embroidery: Select your monogram and follow the appropriate chart for placement. See page 26 for cross-stitch.

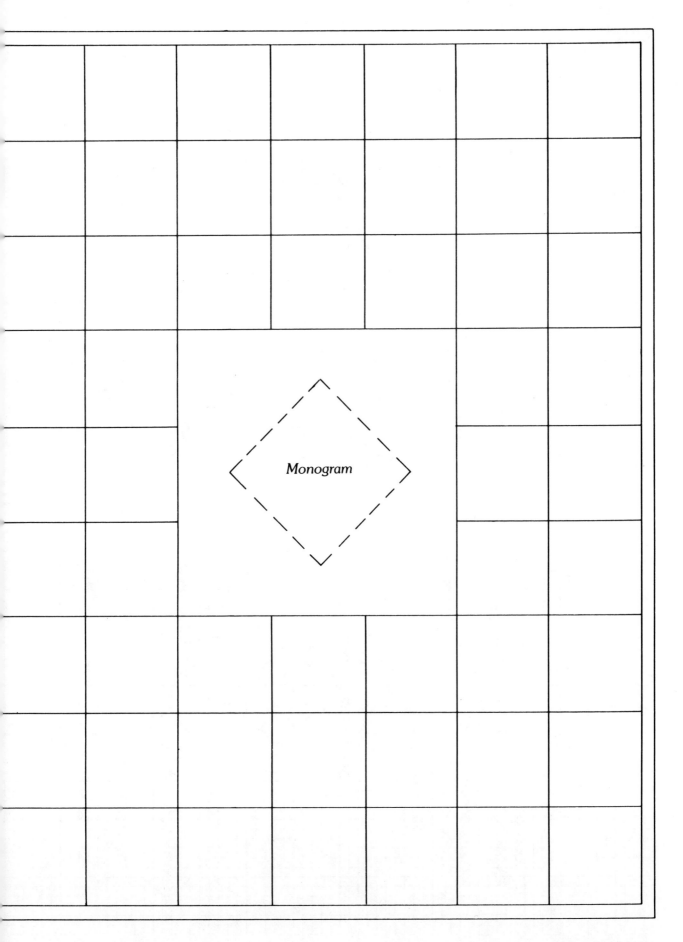

Monogram

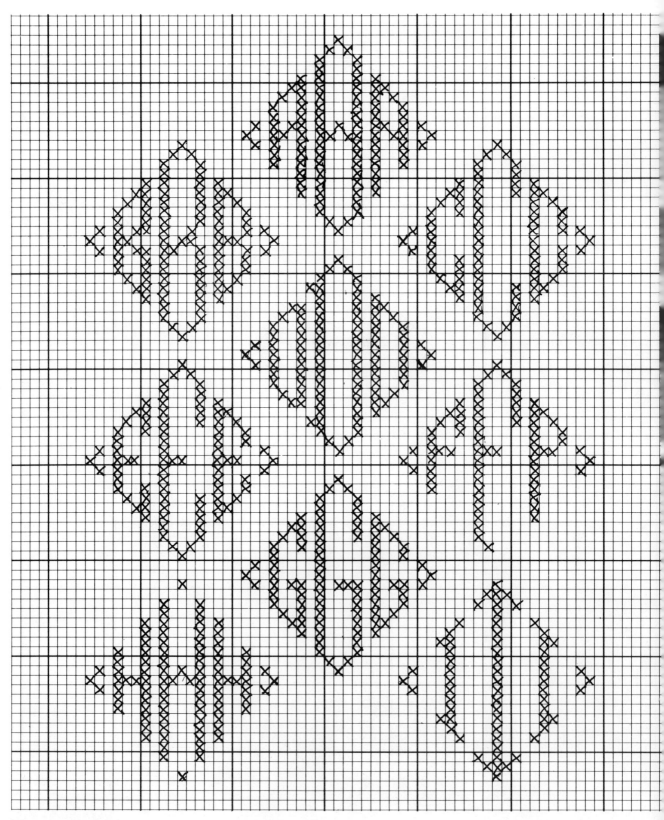

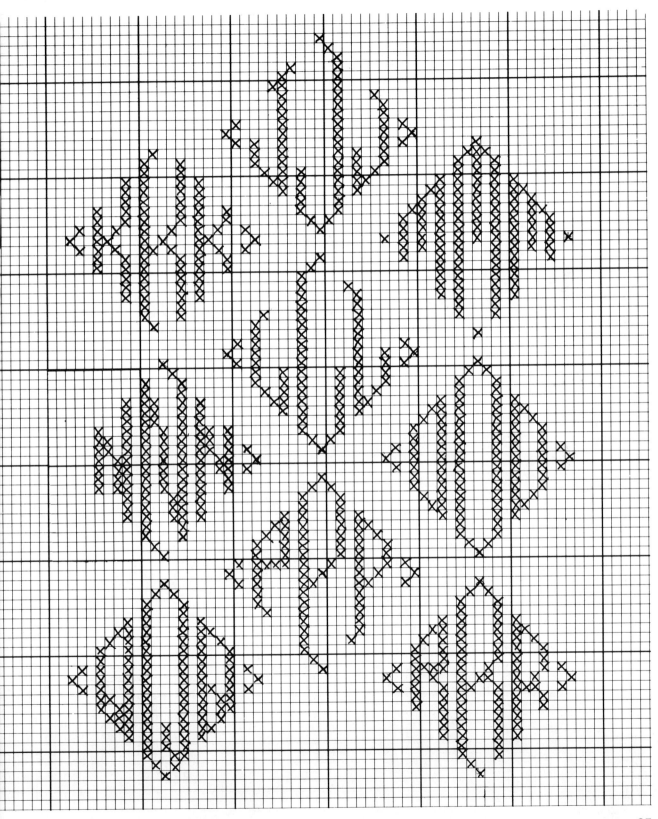

This subtle, herringbone pattern uses 4 colors that combine well to make a soft, elegant afghan. Beginning with white, each color increases in a darker shade of natural to brown. The bulky weight yarn and large needles make this a quick project, and since all the pieces are made individually, it is easy as well. Each section is 5 × 10 inches, and the finished afghan is 48 × 72 inches.

Materials: Phildar Kadischa bulky weight yarn 50-gram balls—15 skeins of each color: #10 blanc (white) A, #60 mouflon (natural) B, #11 Bison (light brown) C, #89 Tabou (brown) D.
Needles: #10
Gauge: 7 sts = 2 inches
         9 rows = 2 inches

Directions

The afghan is made up of equal numbers of rectangular pieces in each color. There are 108 total. Cast on with any color 18 sts. Work stockinette st (k 1 row, p 1 row) for 10 inches. Bind off loosely. Once you have completed all the pieces, they must be carefully arranged. Use the diagram to lay out each row and check as you join them so that all A, B, and C sections are accurately placed.

Join the sections in zigzag rows of 9. Remember that each row will be joined to the row above it, but leaning in the opposite directions. When stitching sections together to create the individual rows, you should keep this in mind.

Once you have 12 rows of 9 pieces, start at the bottom and join each subsequent row. If you block each row before joining them, it will be helpful.

When completed, steam press the wrong side lightly.

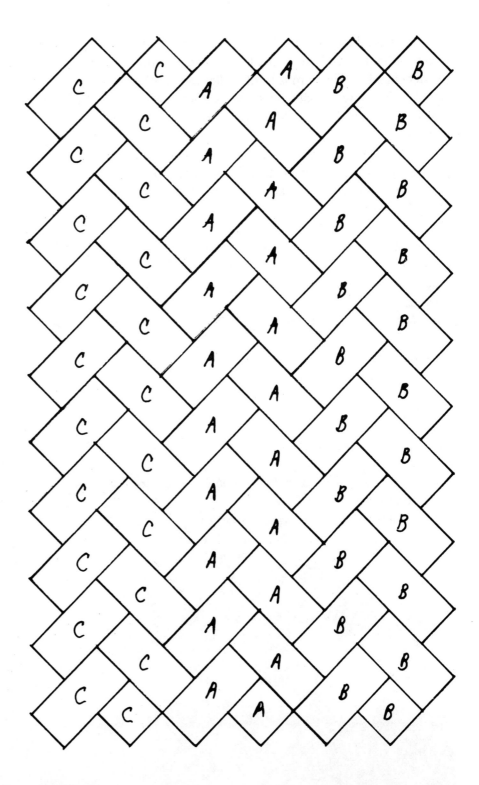

A—Natural
B—Light brown
C—Brown

Quick-to-knit country afghan

A good combination of colors and yarn that work well together is used here to create an unusual country-style blanket. The yarn is a soft bulky weight that is delightful to work with on large needles, which make it quick to knit, while creating an interesting texture.

The squares are knit individually and are then joined with a crochet stitch that frames each one. Each square is 6 × 6 inches, and the finished afghan is 48 × 60 inches.

Materials: Phildar bulky weight Bagherra 50-gram balls—4 skeins each of #67 Noir (black), #08 Beige, gray, 5 skeins #32 Ecru (natural); large-eyed tapestry needle.
Needles: #10½ or #11
Hook: F
Gauge: 3 sts = 1 inch
       4 rows = 1 inch

Directions

You will make 20 squares in each color for a total of 80 squares.
Cast on 18 sts in any color. Each square is done in stockinette st (k 1 row, p 1 row).
Trim: With right side of square facing you, insert crochet hook from front to back in first st of square.

Using matching color, hold yarn in back of work and draw up loop. Continuing to hold yarn in back of work throughout, crochet loosely one row of sl sts evenly along entire outer edge of square. Adjust tension so work will not pull. Break off.

Finish: Block each square by lightly steam pressing the back while adjusting to 6×6-inch finished size. Arrange colors according to diagram.

Using a large-eyed tapestry needle and the color of one of the squares being joined, sew together allowing sl st trim to remain free on right side.

Fringe (optional): Using Ecru, cut several strands double the length desired (6 inches finished size = 12 inches cut strands) plus an extra inch for the knot. Fold the strands in half, and using a crochet hook, pull them through a st in outer edge of afghan. Draw loose ends through lp and pull tightly to form a knot. Tie fringe in 1-inch spacing along entire length of top and bottom edges.

A	D	C	B	A	D	C	B
B	A	D	C	B	A	D	C
C	B	A	D	C	B	A	D
D	C	B	A	D	C	B	A
A	D	C	B	A	D	C	B
B	A	D	C	B	A	D	C
C	B	A	D	C	B	A	D
D	C	B	A	D	C	B	A
A	D	C	B	A	D	C	B
B	A	D	C	B	A	D	C

A—Black
B—Beige
C—Natural
D—Gray

Imagine tucking baby to sleep under a blanket of stars! This easy-to-knit afghan is a perfect weekend project. Done in stockinette with a knit border, the stars and moon are then embroidered on top. You might even enjoy making a small carriage pillow to match.

The finished afghan is 38×47 inches, and the pillow is 12 inches square.

Materials: Bucilla Wonderknit easy-care acrylic 3-oz. skeins—5 skeins navy blue; small amount of pink, white, and yellow (1-2-3 ply Persian-type yarn comes in 12-yard skeins and is good for the embroidered motifs); Stacy's TraceErase (optional for ease of embroidery); embroidery needle.

Needles: #10½

Gauge: 8 sts = 2 inches

13 rows = 2 inches

Directions

Beginning with navy yarn, cast on 110 sts. Work for 3¼ inches in garter st (k each row). Next row, knit 17 sts, then change to stockinette st for 76 sts.

Knit last 17 sts in row.

Continue this pattern (17 sts all knit, 76 sts stockinette, 17 sts all knit) for 44 inches from start. End on right side of work.

Work last 3¼ inches all garter st to finish. Bind off loosely.

Embroidery: It is sometimes difficult to transfer an embroidery design to a knit surface, especially if the background is a dark color. In this case I would recommend a product called Stacy's TraceErase (see page 40).

Simply trace the stars and moon shapes on the TraceErase and pin each one in place on the afghan. You can follow the picture for placement, or the designs can be placed at random. You can then make perfect shapes by following the outline of the drawing. Use a satin stitch and embroider right over the tracing.

When you have finished the entire motif, pull away the excess TraceErase, which will be easy to remove. If there are a few difficult-to-remove strands, use a tweezers.

Finish: Block the stockinette area of the blanket by steam pressing the back. You might want to pad the ironing board when steaming each embroidered element. This afghan is completely washable.

Pillow

Make 2. Cast on 59 stitches and knit 45 rows in stockinette st. Bind off loosely. Stitch front and back pieces together, leaving one side open to insert pillow form. Stitch opening closed.

Checkerboard afghan p. 28

Quick throw p. 142

Apple granny p. 152

Cloudspun p. 44

Stadium blanket p. 128

Country hearts p. 46

Earth-tone throw p. 138

Log cabin p. 130

Navaho afghan p. 54

Baby ripple p. 136

Quick-to-knit country afghan p. 90

Woven rug pattern p. 58

Baby starbursts p. 70

Caribbean calypso p. 78

American beauty p. 101

Embroidery for baby p. 50

Painted desert p. 34

Soft and fluffy baby coverlet p. 149

Mosaic squares p. 74

All-American p. 66

This is a variation of the Star light, star bright afghan. The finished size is 34 inches square. Choose the design from the three presented here and embroider on the center panel.

Materials: Bucilla Wonderknit easy-care acrylic 3-oz. skeins—5 skeins white; 1-2-3 ply Persian-type yarn in a variety of colors for embroidery; Stacy's TraceErase; embroidery needle.
Needles: #10½
Gauge: 8 sts = 2 inches
            13 rows = 2 inches

Directions

Cast on 94 sts. Work for 3½ inches in garter st (knit each row). Next row, knit 17 sts, then change to stockinette st for 60 sts.
Knit last 17 sts in row.
Continue this pattern (17 sts all knit, 60 sts stockinette, 17 sts all knit) for 27 inches from start. End on right side of work.
Work last 3½ inches all garter st to finish. Bind off loosely.
Embroidery: It is sometimes difficult to transfer an embroidery design to a knit surface. Use Stacy's TraceErase and trace the design onto this gauzelike paper. Pin in place on the afghan. Following the outline of the drawing, use a running stitch to embroider right over the tracing.

When you have finished the entire motif, pull away the excess Trace Erase, which will be easy to remove. If there are a few difficult-to-remove strands, use a tweezers.
Finish: Block the stockinette area by steam pressing the back. This afghan is completely washable.

Each square equals 3 inches.

Storybook carriage cover

Each square equals 3 inches.

This delicate rose is embroidered over the stockinette background. The afghan can be made in one of two ways: You can use circular needles to make the entire afghan in one piece, or you might prefer piecing it in the manner of quilt making. In this way, you will knit the long side panels and top and bottom panels separately. The center panel is another piece, and when completed, the pieces are joined with invisible stitches. The finished afghan is 53 × 59 inches.

Materials: Bucilla Softex knitting worsted or wool 4-oz. skeins—6 skeins blue; 3 skeins white; 1-2-3 ply Persian-type yarn—3 skeins each of blue, green, and pink; 2 skeins red; embroidery needle.

Needles: #10

Gauge: 7 sts = 2 inches

            13 rows = 2 inches

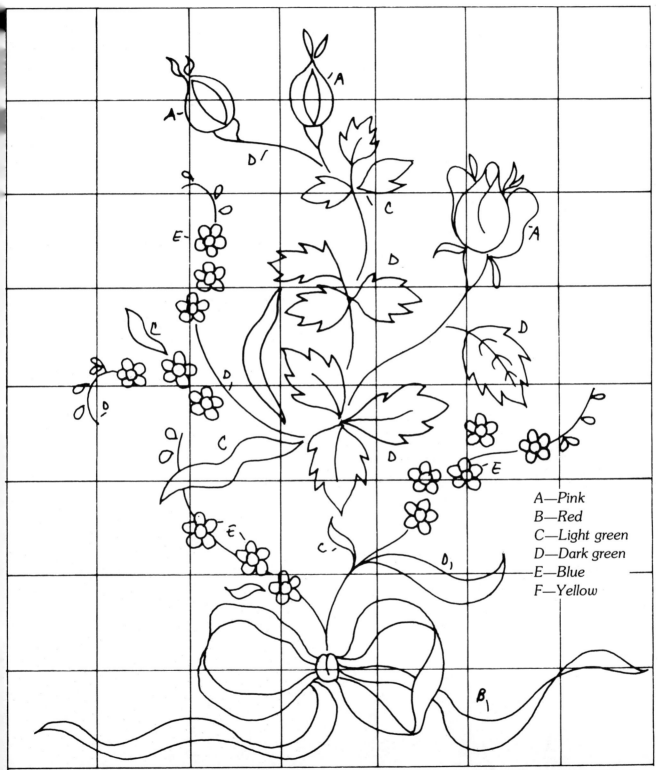

A—Pink
B—Red
C—Light green
D—Dark green
E—Blue
F—Yellow

Each square equals 3¾ inches.

103

Directions

For pieced method: Make 2. With blue, cast on 42 sts. Work all garter stitch (all knit) for 59 inches. Bind off.

With blue, cast on 102 sts. Knit for 12 inches. Bind off. (Make 2.)

Center panel: With white, cast on 102 sts. Work in stockinette st (1 row k, 1 row p) for 35 inches. Bind off loosely.

Joining panels: With right sides facing, join top short panel to top of center panel. Using large-eyed, blunt needle and white yarn, pick up 1 st and pull yarn through. Pick up next st from opposite side. Repeat. Leave 3-inch tail to weave into backstitches.

Next, join remaining short blue panel to opposite end of center panel in the same way. Repeat with side panels, matching stitches as you join them.

Embroidery: Before beginning, lightly steam press center panel from wrong side. Enlarge the design (see page 103). Trace the enlarged design onto the Trace-Erase (see pp. 50 and 52) for easy embroidery. Follow color key and stitch pattern for embroidered design.

Finish: Pad ironing board and lightly steam press back of center embroidered panel.

One-piece method: Using circular needles and blue yarn, cast on 210 stitches. Work in garter st (all knit) for 12 inches.

Continue 35 inches with 12 inches in garter stitch (blue), then change yarn to white for 29 inches in stockinette, ending row with 12 inches in blue garter stitch.

Last 12 inches are worked same as first 12 inches, all knit with blue yarn.

Seed stitch carriage blanket

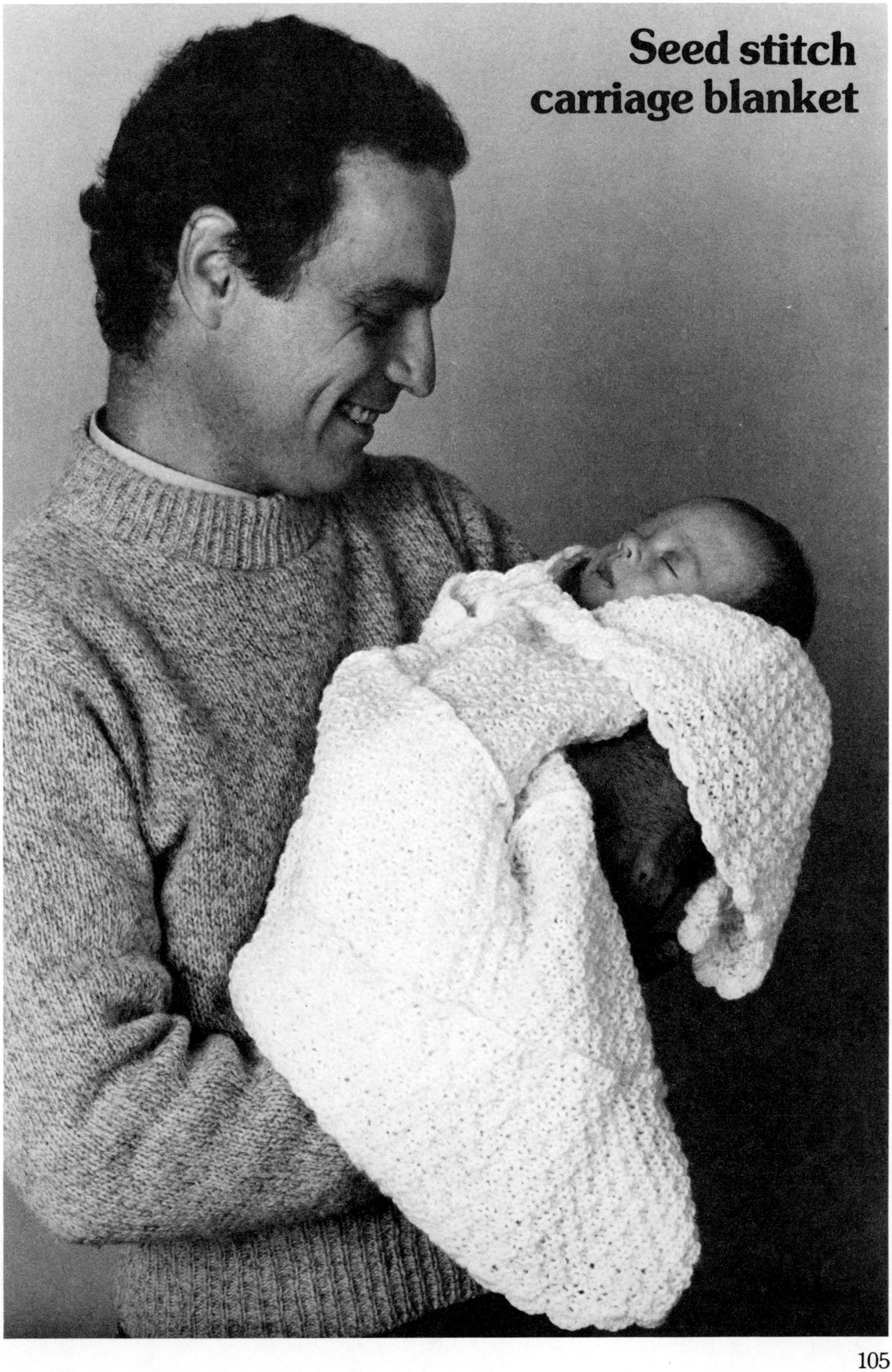

A soft white blanket is always a nice baby gift that can be used in the carriage or for wrapping a newborn baby. The seed stitch is used with a soft washable yarn.

Materials: Phildar 50-gram balls Suffrage #249 white—8 balls.
Needles: #8
Gauge: 4 sts = 1 inch
       6 rows = 1 inch

Directions

Each square is 5 inches. Make 42. Cast on 20 sts.
Row 1: K 2, * p 2, k 2, rep from * across.
Row 2: * p 2, k 2, rep from * across, end p 2.
Row 3: P 2, * k 2, p 2, rep from * across.
Row 4: * k 2, p 2, rep from * across and end k 2.
Rep these 4 rows for pattern until piece measures 5 inches from start; end pattern row 2 or 4. Bind off.
Finishing: Block squares to 5 inches. Single crochet from wrong side to attach squares. There should be 6 squares across and 7 down for a finished size of approximately 30 × 35 inches. Single crochet around entire outer edge.

Getting started in crochet

Most of the projects made in crochet can be achieved with a few basic stitches. All the work starts with a chain made up of a series of loops on a crochet hook. Unlike knitting, which is done on two, three, and sometimes four needles, crocheting is done on a single hook. Hooks come in various sizes. The size you use will depend on the yarn, pattern, and item.

Most yarn used for knitting can also be used for crocheting. However, the very fine crochet cotton is best for the fine lacy items made with crochet stitches rather than knitting.

Chain stitch

All projects here begin with the chain stitch.

1. Make a slip knot by taking yarn about 2 inches from end and winding it once around your middle three fingers.

2. Pull a length of yarn through the loop around your fingers. Put this new loop on your crochet hook and pull tight.

3. With yarn wound over left-hand fingers, pass the hook under the yarn on your index finger and catch a strand with the hook.

4. Draw the yarn through the loop already on the hook to make one chain stitch. Repeat steps 3 and 4 for as many chain stitches as needed. If you hold the chain as close to the hook as possible with the thumb and index finger of your left hand, the chain will be even.

Single crochet

The beginning of every project in crochet is a row of a specific number of chain stitches. These are the basis of the piece, just as the cast-on row is the basis of a knit piece.

At the beginning of every row, an extra chain stitch is made. This is counted as the first stitch of the row and is called the turning chain.

1. After making the initial chain, insert hook in second chain from the hook (the skipped chain is the turning chain) and bring the yarn over the hook from back to front (clockwise). Pull the yarn over through the chain so you have two loops on the hook. (Note that in these instructions, each chain stitch is simply called a chain. Where a string of chain stitches is being discussed, it is known by the numbers of stitches—for example, "first ch 5" means the first group of 5 chain stitches in a row.)

2. Wind the yarn around the hook again and draw the hook with its 3rd loop through the two loops already on the hook. You have made one single crochet (sc).

3. Continue to work a single crochet in each chain stitch. At the end of the row, make one chain (ch 1) and turn your work around from right to left so the reverse is facing you.

4. The turning chain stitch counts as the first stitch. Work the next single crochet by inserting your hook through the top loop of the next stitch in the previous row. Wind the yarn over the hook (yo) and draw it through the stitch. Yarn over and through two loops on hook. Continue to work a single crochet in each stitch across row. Chain 1 and turn.

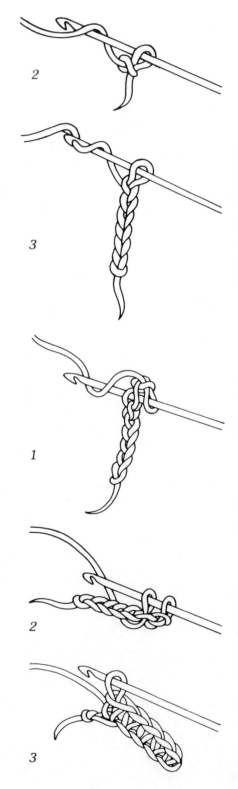

Fastening off

At the end of all required rows or rounds, cut the yarn with a tail of 2 or 3 inches and draw it through the last loop at the end of the row. Pull tightly and weave it into the fabric with a yarn needle. Sometimes the tail is used to sew pieces together. Cut off yarn according to how the piece will be used. Sometimes you may need more to sew with.

Double crochet

1. With your foundation chain made, bring yarn over hook and insert hook in 4th chain from hook.
2. Yarn over hook. Draw through chain. There are 3 loops on hook.
3. Yarn over hook. Draw through 2 loops on hook. There are now 2 loops on hook.
4. Yarn over hook. Draw yarn through the last 2 loops on hook. One double crochet is completed. Insert hook into next stitch in foundation chain, and repeat steps 2, 3, and 4.
   Once you've worked a double crochet in every chain across the row, ch 3 and turn. This turning chain of 3 chain stitches counts as one double crochet beginning the next row.
5. Skip first stitch and work double crochet (dc) in top loop of each double crochet across.
6. Work double crochet in first stitches of ch 3 (turning chain).

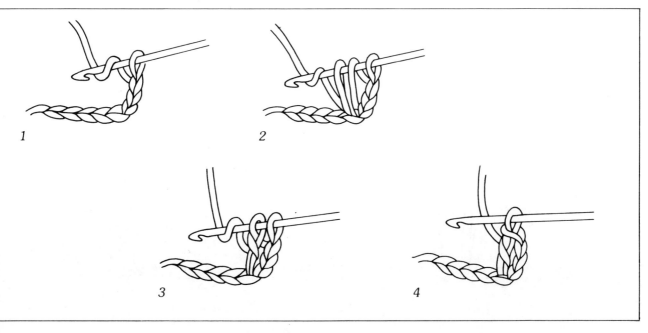

1

2

3

4

Half double crochet

Make a foundation chain.

1. Yarn over hook and insert hook through loop of third chain from hook.

2. Yarn over hook. Draw yarn through the chain so there are 3 loops on hook.

3. Yarn over hook. Draw through all 3 loops to complete half double crochet (hdc).

Continue to do this in each chain across row. At end of row, ch 2 to turn. Slip first stitch and work first half double crochet into each half double crochet across. Last hdc in row is worked in turning ch. Ch 2 to turn.

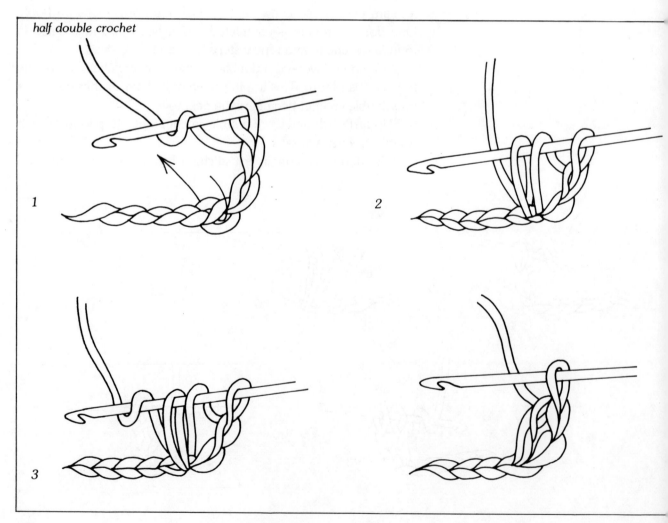

half double crochet

1

2

3

Treble or triple crochet

Make a foundation chain.

With 1 loop on your hook, put the yarn over the hook twice. Insert hook in 5th chain from the hook, yarn over hook and pull loop through. Yarn over, draw through 2 loops at once 3 times.

At end of row, ch 4 and turn. This turning chain of 4 is the first triple crochet (tr) of the next row.

Turning

Depending on the crochet stitch you are working, you will need a number of chain stitches at the end of each row to bring your work into position for the next row. For a single crochet, you will ch 1 to turn; for a half double crochet, you will ch 2; for a double crochet, you will ch 3; and for a treble or triple crochet, ch 4.

treble crochet

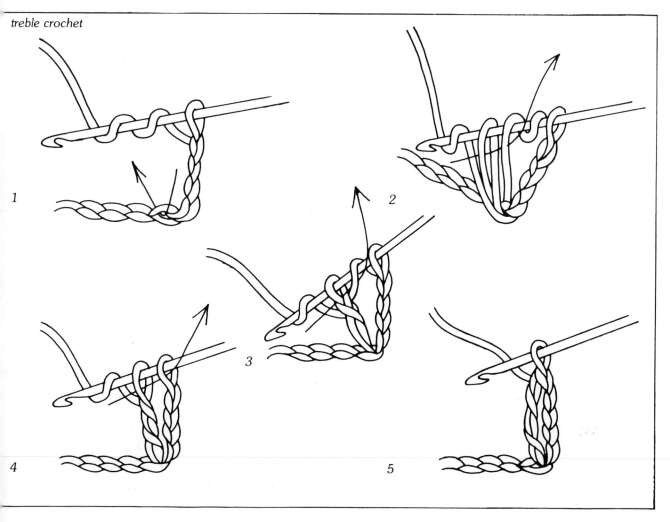

1 2 3 4 5

Slip stitch

slip stitch

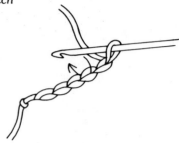

Insert hook into chain. Yarn over hook and draw through both stitch and loop on hook in one motion. This completes one slip stitch (sl st). A slip stitch is used to join a chain in order to form a ring.

Joining rounds

If you are making a hat, for example, work to the end of the round as per directions given for the specific project. Then join by inserting hook into top loop of first stitch on same round you have been working, and work slip stitch. In this way you join the first and last stitches of the round.

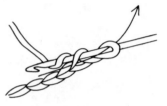

Working in spaces

In crocheted work that is lacier and contains openwork, often a stitch in the preceding row is skipped; instead, you will be instructed to chain across the gap. Sometimes your pattern asks you to work stitches in a space instead of in a stitch. In that case, insert your hook through the gap or space (sp) rather than through a stitch in the preceding row. Often several stitches are worked in one space, as a way of increasing stitches.

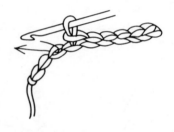

increasing single crochet

Increasing single crochet

When a pattern calls for an increase of a single crochet, work 2 stitches in 1 stitch.

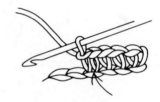

Decreasing single crochet

When a pattern calls for a decrease of a single crochet, pull up a loop in 1 stitch, then pull up a loop in the next stitch so there are 3 loops on your hook. Yarn over hook and draw through all 3 loops at once.

decreasing single crochet

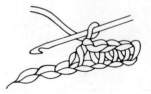

Crocheting tips

Yarn

Most yarn used for knitting can also be used for crochet projects. However, the very fine crochet cotton will enable you to achieve a lacy motif that is more delicate than that done with traditional knitting yarns.

As with knitting, it is best to buy the amount you need to finish a project. Often the colors change slightly from one dye lot to another, and if you run out in the middle of a project, you may not find the exact yarn you need to finish.

Gauge

Make a swatch approximately 4 × 4 inches using the yarn, hook, and stitch pattern recommended. This will give you a chance to see the yarn made up as well as to check the gauge before beginning the project. Count the recommended stitches for the given inches and mark with pins at beginning and end. With a tape measure on the flat swatch, check to see if they correspond. If you have fewer stitches per inch than the pattern calls for, your work is too loose. Change to a smaller hook. If the stitches measure more than they should, then go up one hook size. Make another swatch to be sure the gauge is correct, and adjust accordingly.

Crocheting abbreviations

beg—beginning
bet—between
ch—chain
dc—double crochet
dec—decrease
grp—group
hdc—half double crochet
inc—increase
L—left
lp—loop
pat—pattern
R—right
rem—remaining
rep—repeat
rnd—round
sc—single crochet
sk—skip
sl st—slip stitch
sp—space
st—stitch
tog—together
tr—treble or triple crochet
yo—yarn over hook
*—repeat what comes after
() work directions in parentheses as many times as specified after parentheses. For example: (dc 1, ch 1) 3 times.

Granny squares

Although the pieces that make up granny afghans are often called "squares," they come in a variety of motifs. They may be squares, hexagons, circles, octagons, or stars. Some even come scalloped. These motifs are joined, and the resulting combination of stitches and colors determines the size and design of the completed afghan.

Beginning in the center, the motif is increased in size as you work outwards. The shapes are created by the combination of stitches used. Some grannies are lacy and filled with "holes"; others are more solidly constructed. Some stitches even create a design in the center of the motif from which other patterns emanate.

The granny afghan is probably the most popular form of crochet as it is decorative and versatile. Using the individual shapes, you can make all sorts of blankets as well as place mats, pillows, and clothing. The number of motifs and size of each determines the size of the finished project.

As with our early American quilts, the granny afghan demonstrates the practical value of using leftover material to create a warm cover. Although design was often a secondary consideration, today we find granny-square afghans among the most beautifully designed. With the availability of so many different kinds of yarns and colors, the potential for a project is limitless.

Furthermore, this form of crocheting is easy to work and carry along. The individual pieces can be thrown in your purse for on-the-go crafting. Is it any wonder that "granny" has become the very symbol of crochet in this country?

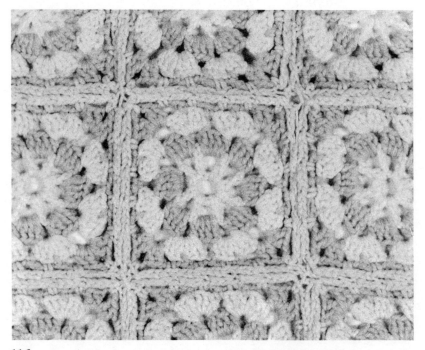

Baby granny

Pretty enough for any baby, this little cover is designed for the bassinet or carriage. To enlarge, just add more rows of granny squares.

This is a quick and easy project done in washable 4-ply acrylic. The colors used here are mint green and white for the wheel pattern, which is surrounded and joined together with bright pink. The finished afghan is 23×32 inches.

Materials: Coats and Clark Wintuk 3½-oz. skeins—2 skeins mint green, 2 skeins white, 1 skein pink.
Hooks: F and J (for border)
Gauge: Each motif = 4½ inches square

Directions

Make 35.
Color sequence: White (A), green (B), pink (C).
Using A, make a ch of 8 and join into a ring with sl st into first ch.
Rnd 1: Using A, ch 6, * 1 dc into ring, ch 3, rep from *6 times more, join with a sl st to 3rd of first ch-6. Break off A.
Rnd 2: Join B to any sp, ch 3, 3 dc into same sp, * ch 2, 4 dc into next sp, rep from * 6 more times, ch 2, join with a sl st to 3rd of first ch-3. Break off B.
Rnd 3: Join A to any sp, ch 3, 5 dc into same sp, * ch 1, 6 dc into next sp, ch 3, 6 dc into next sp, rep from * twice more, ch 1, 6 dc into next sp, ch 3. Break off A.
Rnd 4: Join B to a ch-1 sp, * ch 3, sc between 3rd and 4th dc of grp, ch 3 (2 dc, ch 3, 2 dc) into ch-3 sp, ch 3, sc bet 3rd and 4th dc of grp, ch 3, 1 sc into ch-1 sp, rep from * 3 more times, omitting last sc and join with sl st to first ch. Fasten off.
Finish: With color C, sew motifs tog with 5 squares across and 7 rows down, sewing through back loops only of sc's on rnd 4.
Border: With C, work 1 rnd sc around afghan. Change to J hook. Working from left to right, work sc in each sc around (crab st). End off.

Star afghan

The motif for this afghan is a hexagonal shape with a star in the center. Each motif can be worked up quickly, and you can use any color combination. This is also the perfect project for using up your scraps. Make every motif a different color combination or choose one color for the background with a different color for each center. The finished project is 48 × 63 inches.

Materials: Bernat Berella "4" knitting worsted 4-oz. skeins—6 skeins white (A), 7 skeins purple (B).
Hook: H
Gauge: Each motif is approximately 3 inches.

Directions

First motif: With color A, ch 4, sl st in first ch to form ring.
Rnd 1: Ch 3, *(yo hook, insert hook in ring and pull up a ½-inch lp) 4 times, yo hook and through all 9 lps on hook, ch 1 to fasten; ch 4. Rep from * 5 times, insert hook in ch 1 at top of first cluster, pull through a lp, break off A. Draw color B through 2 lps on hook.
Rnd 2: With B, sl st in ch-4 sp, ch 3 (counts as 1 dc); working over ends of white and purple, make 4 dc in ch-4 sp, * ch 3, 5 dc in next ch-4 sp, rep from * 4 times, ch 3, sl st in top of starting ch. Fasten off.
Second motif: Rnd 1 is worked same as for first motif.
Rnd 2: With B, sl st in ch-4 sp, ch 3, 4 dc in ch-4 sp, ch 1; holding first motif in back of work, wrong sides tog, sl st in any ch-3 sp of first motif, ch 1.
5 dc in next ch-4 sp, ch 1, sl st in next ch-3 sp of first motif, ch 1, 5 dc in next ch-4 sp, ch 3.
Work to end of rnd as for first motif.
Row 1: Work 15 more motifs, joining to preceding motif as for second motif (17 motifs).
Row 2: Work as for first motif through rnd 1.
Rnd 2: With B, sl st in ch-4 sp, ch 3, 4 dc in ch 4 sp, ch 1.

Holding first motif of first row in back of work, with wrong sides together, join to ch-3 sp before you join first two motifs of first row. Ch 1, 5 dc in next ch-4 sp, ch 1, join in sl st to join first and second motifs of first

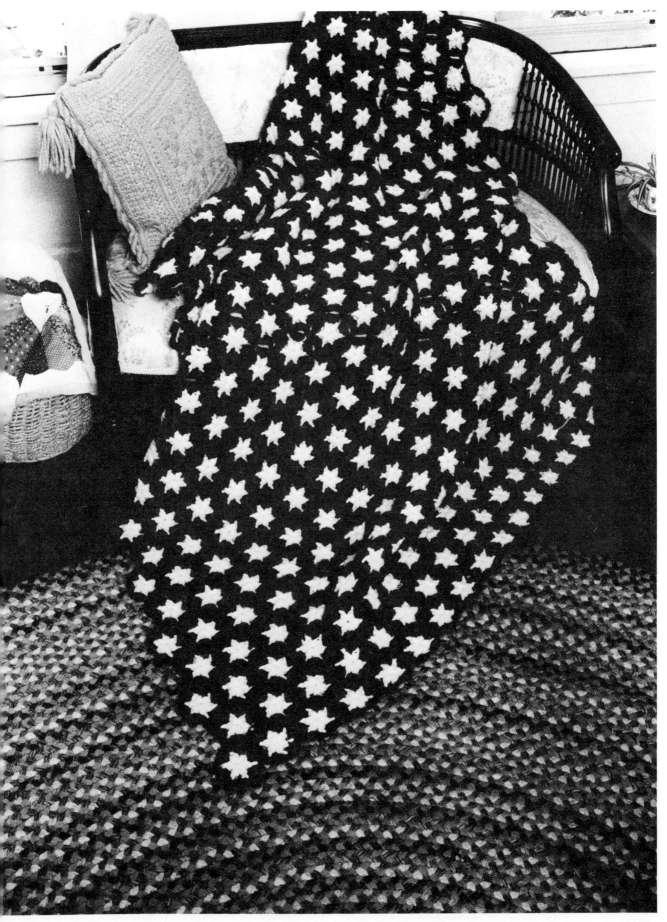

row, ch 1, 5 dc in next ch-4 sp, ch 1, join to next ch-3 sp of second motif of first row, ch 1, work to end of rnd as for first motif.

Work second motif, joining to first free sp of first motif, to next joining st (bet first motif of second row and second motif of first row), to next joining st (bet second and third motifs of first row). Finish motif as before.

Continue in this way, joining 16 motifs of 2nd row to 17 motifs of 1st row.

Alternate rows of 17 motifs with rows of 16 motifs, and work until there are 14 rows of 17 motifs and 13 rows of 16 motifs.

Finish: With B, sc around afghan, making 1 sc in each dc and 1 sc in each sp. Join to first sc. Fasten off.

Blocking: Steam press wrong side lightly. You may find that a well-padded ironing board, a damp cloth, and a dry iron work best.

Fringe: (Make 34.) Wind A around a 2½-inch piece of cardboard 10 times. Tie strands tog at one edge of cardboard. Cut the strands at the opposite edge. Wind a separate strand of A several times around all strands just below top of tassel. Hide ends inside fringe.

Tie a fringe to each free ch-3 sp across the top and bottom of the afghan. Tuck ends inside, and trim fringe evenly.

Persian granny

The traditional granny-square afghan is always a favorite and this time it's presented in a combination of earth tones of browns, grays, and natural. Every square is worked the same; only the colors change to create an interesting pattern.

The finished afghan is 48×54 inches. If you want to add a border, there will be an additional 2 inches all around, making it 50×56 inches.

Materials: Phildar Leader knitting worsted 3½-oz. balls—4 balls sienna ("Brandy" reddish brown), 3 balls white, 1 ball ochre ("Mahari" yellowish brown), 4 balls black, and 3 balls "Buffalo" gray.
Hook: H
Gauge: 1 rnd = 1 inch
       1 granny square = 6 inches

Directions

Follow the color chart and make the following: 14 A, 26 B, 26 C, and 6 D. There are a total of 73 squares.

	Square A	Square B	Square C	Square D
Rnd 1	Sienna	Black	White	Black
Rnd 2	Gray	Ochre	Black	Gray
Rnd 3	White	Sienna	Sienna	Sienna
Rnd 4	White	Sienna	Sienna	Sienna
Rnd 5	White	Gray	Black	Ochre
Rnd 6	White	Gray	Black	Gray

For color specified in column A for first round, sienna, ch 4, join with a sl st to form a ring.

Rnd 1: Continuing with sienna, ch 3; working over yarn end, 2 dc in ring (ch 2, 3 dc in ring) 3 times. Ch 2, join with a sl st in beg ch-3. Finish off.

Rnd 2: Without turning, join gray (second color) with a sl st in any ch-2 sp, ch 3 (2 dc, ch 2, 3 dc) in same sp as joining. You have made the first corner. *(3 dc, ch 2, 3 dc) in next ch-2 sp (corner made); ch 1. Rep from * twice more. Join with a sl st in beg ch-3. Finish off.

Rnd 3: Without turning, join white with a sl st in any ch-2 corner sp; ch 3 (2 dc, ch 2, 3 dc) in same sp as joining; *3 dc, ch 1 between next two 3-dc grps for side ch 1, (3 dc, ch 2, 3 dc) in next corner sp. Rep from * twice more. 3 dc bet next 2 grps of 3-dc for last side; ch 1, join with a sl st in beg ch-3. Do not finish off.

Rnd 4: Do not turn; sl st in each of next 2 dc and into corner sp; ** ch 3 (2 dc, ch 2, 3 dc) in same sp; * 3 dc, ch 1 bet each pair of 3-dc grps along side ch 1 (3 dc, ch 2, 3 dc) in next corner sp; rep from * twice more. 3 dc bet each pair of 3-dc grps along last side; ch 1, join with a sl st in top of beg ch-3. Finish off**.

Rnd 5: Do not turn; continuing with white, sl st in any corner sp. Work as for rnd 4 from ** to **.

Rnd 6: Rep rnd 5. Weave all ends into back of work.

When following the directions, remember that each square group is made up of slightly different colors. You will fasten off and change colors as indicated on the chart for granny squares A, B, C, and D.

Finish: Arrange the squares according to the diagram. With right sides together and matching sts on both squares, sew together with an overcast st in outer lps only across side. Begin and end with one corner st. Join squares in rows; then join rows as you did the squares.

Border: With right sides facing, join black yarn with a sl st in any corner sp of afghan.

Rnd 1: Ch 3 (2 dc, ch 2, 3 dc) in same sp as joining along each side edge, work 3 dc bet each pair of 3-dc grps, and in each corner sp of squares on each side of joinings, and in each rem corner sp of the afghan. Work (3 dc, ch 2, 3 dc), join with a sl st in top of beg ch-3. Fasten off.

Rnd 2: Work in same manner as squares, 3 dc bet each pair of 3-dc grps along sides, ch 1, and (3 dc, ch 2, 3 dc) in each corner sp. Fasten off. Weave loose ends of yarn under back of afghan.

C	B	C	B	C	B	C	B
B	C	B	C	B	C	B	C
C	B	A	A	A	A	C	B
B	C	A	D	D	A	B	C
C	B	A	D	D	A	B	C
B	C	A	D	D	A	B	C
C	B	A	A	A	A	C	B
B	C	B	C	B	C	B	C
C	B	C	B	C	B	C	B

Assembly diagram

Stadium blanket

Make a warm blanket to take with you to outdoor sports events. This stadium blanket is a handy size to fold up and keep in the car as well.

The large granny square is worked quickly on a #13 hook and it takes only one bag (8 skeins) of 4-oz. yarn. The variegated yarn makes this blanket colorful without the problems of joining different yarns.

Materials: Tahki Ambrosia II—1 bag (8 skeins) wool, color purple.
Hook: #13

Directions

Chain 5, join with sl st to form a ring.
Rnd 1: Ch 3, 2 dc in ring sp, * ch 3, 3 dc in ring. Repeat from * twice more, end with ch 3, sl st in 3rd st of 1st ch-3.
Rnd 2: Sl st to first sp, ch 3 (2 dc, ch 3, 3 dc) in same sp (corner), * ch 1, sk 3 dc (3 dc, ch 3, 3 dc) in next sp, repeat from * twice, end with a ch 1, sl st in top of ch-3.
Rnd 3: Sl st to corner sp, ch 3 (2 dc, ch 3, 3 dc) in same sp, * ch 1, 3 dc in next sp, ch 1 (3 dc, ch 3, 3 dc) in corner sp, repeat from *, end with a ch 1, 3 dc in next sp, ch 1, sl st in top of ch-3.
Rnd 4: Sl st to corner of sp, ch 3 (2 dc, ch 3, 3 dc) in same sp, * ch 1, 3 dc in first sp, ch 1, 3 dc in 2nd sp, ch 1 (3 dc, ch 3, 3 dc) in corner sp, repeat from * around, end with a ch 1 (3 dc in next sp) 2 times, ch 1, sl st in top of ch 3.
Rnd 5: Sl st to corner sp, ch 3 (2 dc, ch 3, 3 dc) in same sp, * (ch 1, 3 dc in next sp) 3 times, ch 1 (3 dc, ch 3, 3 dc) in corner sp, repeat from * around, end with a (ch 1, 3 dc in next sp) 3 times, ch 1, sl st in top of ch-3.

Continue working as for rnd 5, adding one more group of 3 dc (or 4 grps in total round), on each side of blanket every round. Fasten off when yarn runs out. 24 rounds should equal 48 inches.

Log cabin

Everyone seems to love the log cabin design whether it's found in quilts or afghans. This is a very easy project to crochet, and there are an infinite number of color combinations to choose from. Each square is made individually with a border around the block. When the squares are complete, they are all stitched together. The finished project is 54 × 76 inches. If you want to make it larger, just add the desired number of rows. This project is sure to become an heirloom.

Materials: Bernat Berella "4" knitting worsted 4-oz. skeins—5 skeins rose (A), 6 skeins black (B), 9 skeins pink (C), 5 skeins burgundy (D), 8 skeins light gray (E), 6 skeins lavender (F).
Hook: H
Gauge: Each square is 12 inches.

Directions

Refer to diagram for color chart sequence.
Center: With A (rose), ch 15.
Rnd 1: 1 sc in 3rd ch from hook; (ch 1, sk 1, ch 1, sc in next ch) 6 times.
Row 2: Ch 2, turn. 1 sc in lst ch 1 sp (ch 1, 1 sc in next ch 1 sp) 5 times; ch 1, 1 sc in sp under ch 2 at end of row.
Rows 3 through 14: Repeat row 2 twelve times. At end of row 14, change to color B (black) in last sc.
To change colors: Work last sc in row until there are 2 loops on hook. Leave 4-inch ends and finish off color being used. With new color, yo and draw through 2 loops on hook. You now have a color change.

B band
Row 1: Ch 2, turn; working back across row just worked, 1 sc in lst ch 1 sp; (ch 1, 1 sc in next ch 1 sp) 5 times; ch 1, work (1 sc, ch 2, 1 sc) in ch 2 sp at end of row for corner.
  Continuing across side edge of A center, work (ch 1, skip next row, 1 sc in next row) 6 times; ch 1, sk last row, 1 sc in beg ch of foundation chain.

Row 2: Ch 2, turn; work (1 sc, ch 1) in each ch 1 sp to ch 2 sp at corner; work (1 sc, ch 2, 1 sc) in corner sp.

Work (ch 1, 1 sc) in each ch 1 sp across, ending ch 1, 1 sc in sp under turning ch.

Rows 3 through 7: Rep row 2 five times. At end of row 7, change to color C (pink) in last sc.

C band

Row 1: Ch 1, do not turn. Working across ends of B rows and along beg row of A center (1 sc in next row, ch 1, sk next row) 3 times; 1 sc in 1st sc of A center; (ch 1, 1 sc in next ch 1 sp) 6 times. Ch 1, work (1 sc, ch 2, 1 sc) in ch 2 sp at corner. Working across side edge of A center and ends of B (black) band (ch 1, 1 sc in next row, sk next row) 6 times; (ch 1, 1 sc in next row) twice (1 row of each color); (ch 1, sk next row, 1 sc in next row) 3 times.

Rows 2 through 7: Repeat rows 2 through 7 of B band (black). At end of row 7, change to D band (burgundy) in last sc.

D band

On first row, you will be working across ends of C band (pink).

Rnd 1: Ch 2, do not turn; (1 sc in next row, ch 1, sk next row) 3 times; ch 1, 1 sc in turning ch sp at beg of next color band.

Work (ch 1, 1 sc in next ch 1 sp) in each ch 1 sp to corner; ch 1, work (1 sc, ch 2, 1 sc) in corner sp; work (ch 1, 1 sc in next ch 1 sp) in each ch 1 sp to beg of next color band; ch 1, 1 sc in 1st row (at end of next color band); (ch 1, sk next row, 1 sc in next row) 3 times.

Rows 2 through 7: Repeat rows 2 through 7 of B band (black). At end of row 7, change to E (light gray) in last sc.

E band

On first row, you will be working across ends of D band (burgundy) and along last row of C band (pink). Work same as D band (burgundy). At end of last row, change to B band (black) in last sc.

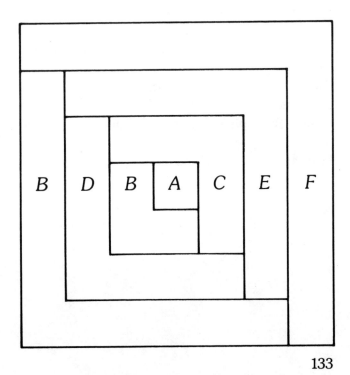

B band

On first row, you will be working across ends of E band (light gray) and along last row of D band (burgundy). At end of last row, change to F (lavender) in last sc.

F band

On first row, you will be working across ends of B band (black) and along last row of E (light gray). Work same as D band (burgundy). At end of last row, finish off.

Make 20 blocks.

Joining blocks: Follow diagram and arrange squares as shown. To join, hold 2 squares with right sides together, and sew or sc blocks tog with 4 squares across and 5 squares down. Join the squares in rows and then join the rows.

Edging: With right sides facing, join B (black) with sl st in any outer corner sp of afghan.

Rnd 1: Ch 1, work (1 sc, ch 2, 1 sc, ch 1) in same sp; work (1 sc, ch 1) in each ch sp of squares outside borders, and in each rem corner sp work (1 sc, ch 2, 1 sc, ch 1). Join with sl st in beg sc.

Rnd 2: Ch 1, turn; sl st into ch 1 sp, ch 1; 1 sc in same sp, ch 1. Work (1 sc, ch 1) in each ch 1 sp around. In each corner sp, work (1 sc, ch 2, 1 sc, ch 1). Join with a sl st in beg sc.

Rep rnd 2 twice more. Turn and join with a sl st in any corner sp.

Rnd 5: Ch 1 (1 sc, ch 2, 1 sc, ch 1) in same space. Complete rnd in same manner as rnd 2.

Rnds 6 through 8: Repeat rnd 2 three times. At end of rnd 8, finish off.

Finish: Weave in all ends, and if necessary, block around border.

Assembly diagram

Baby ripple

A soft, luxuriously warm blanket, this zigzag pattern is worked in 100% wool. It will keep baby warm and snug on outdoor outings in the carriage. The popular pinnacle crochet stitch uses three colors here in 1-inch bands of white, blue, and navy. The finished afghan is 24 × 34 inches.

Materials: Phildar Suffrage wool worsted 50-gram balls—4 skeins of each color: navy, blue, white.
Hook: F
Gauge: 14 sc = 2½ inches

Directions

The color sequence is: navy (A), blue (B), white (C). There are 12 groups of these 3 colors.
Using A, ch 169, ch 2, turn.
Row 1: Sc into 3rd ch from hook. * Sc into each of next 5 ch, skip 2, ch 1, sc into each of next 5 ch, 3 sc into next ch, repeat from * to end, but end with 2 sc into last ch, instead of 3.
Row 2: Ch 1, sc into same place, * sc into each of next 5 sc, skip 2 sc, 1 sc into each of next 5 sc, 3 sc into next sc, rep from * to end, but ending with 2 sc into second from last ch and 2 sc in last chain.
Rep row 2 throughout, working 2 more rows in A, then 4 rows in B, and 4 rows in C to end.

You might like to sc along top and bottom edges in one of the colors.

Earth-tone throw

Earth tones are used to make this checkerboard design in granny squares. Each square is quick and easy to make. Follow the diagram to join them. The subtle colors blend nicely, yet contrast in a dramatic way. The finished afghan is 49 × 63 inches.

Materials: Bucilla Spectator sportyarn 2-oz. skeins —5 skeins charcoal (A), 10 skeins natural (B), 2 skeins blue (C), 2 skeins terra cotta (rust) (D).
Hook: H
Gauge: 1 motif = 6½–7 inches

Directions

Make the following number of squares in each color: 56 A, 91 B, 24 C, and 18 D.
Begin with ch 7, sl st in first ch to form ring.
Rnd 1: Ch 2 (counts as 1 dc), 2 dc in ring, ch 3. (3 dc in ring, ch 3) 3 times; sl st in top of ch 2 at beg of round.
Rnd 2: Ch 2, dc in each of next 2 dc, 2 dc, ch 3, 2 dc in corner sp (dc in each of next 3 dc, 2 dc, ch 3, 2 dc in corner sp) 3 times; sl st in top of ch 2.
Rnd 3: Ch 2, dc in each of next 4 dc, 2 dc, ch 3, 2 dc in corner sp (dc in each of next 7 dc, 2 dc, ch 3, 2 dc in corner sp) 3 times; dc in last 2 dc, sl st in top of ch 2.
Rnd 4: Ch 2, dc in each of next 6 dc, 2 dc, ch 3, 2 dc in corner sp (dc in each of next 11 dc, 2 dc, ch 3, 2 dc in corner sp) 3 times; dc in last 4 dc, sl st in top of ch 2.
Rnd 5: Ch 2, dc in each of next 8 dc, 2 dc, ch 3, 2 dc in corner sp (dc in each of next 15 dc, 2 dc, ch 3, 2 dc in corner sp) 3 times; dc in last 6 dc, sl st in top of ch 2.
Rnd 6: Ch 2, dc in each of next 10 dc, 2 dc, ch 3, 2 dc in corner sp (dc in each of next 19 dc, 2 dc, ch 3, 2 dc in corner sp) 3 times, dc in last 8 dc, sl st in top of ch 2. Fasten off.
Finish: Arrange squares as shown in diagram. Sc squares tog from wrong side, working 1 sc through each pair of corresponding dc, picking up back lps of dc only and working 1 sc in corner sps.

Border: With B, work 6 rnds of dc around afghan, working in back lps of motif sts on first rnd. At corners, work 2 dc, ch 3, 2 dc in corner sp each rnd. Join each rnd with sl st in first dc. With A, work 6 rnds of dc in same way. With A, work 1 rnd sl st all around. End off.

Blocking: Lightly steam the back of afghan to block.

A	B	A	B	A	B	A
B	D	B	D	B	D	B
A	B	A	B	A	B	A
B	C	B	C	B	C	B
A	B	A	B	A	B	A
B	D	B	D	B	D	B
A	B	A	B	A	B	A
B	C	B	C	B	C	B
A	B	A	B	A	B	A

A—Charcoal
B—Natural
C—Blue
D—Rust

Quick throw

This is one project you'll be able to whip up in no time. It's made of one ever increasing granny square. It's perfect for a lap covering on chilly nights.

The finished afghan is 60 inches square.

Materials: Bernat Berella sportyarn 100-gram balls —5 skeins red, 3 skeins gold, 4 skeins blue.
Hook: J
Gauge: 16 sts (4 grps of 3 dc, ch 1) = 6 inches

Directions

Rnd 1: Beg at center with A (red), ch 3, work 2 dc in 3rd ch from hook (counts as 3 dc), ch 2, * 3 dc in same ch, ch 2, repeat from * twice. Join with a sl st in top of starting ch (4 grps of 3 dc).
Rnd 2: Ch 3, 2 dc in joining sl st (half corner), ch 1, * 3 dc, ch 2, 3 dc in next sp (corner), ch 1, rep from * twice, half corner of 3 dc in last sp, ch 2, sl st in top of starting ch 3 (8 grps of 3 dc) (4 corners).

Rnd 3: Ch 3, 2 dc in joining sl st, ch 1 (half corner); * 3 dc in next ch-1 sp, ch 1, corner of 3 dc, ch 2, 3 dc in next corner sp, ch 1.
Repeat from * twice, 3 dc in next ch-1 sp, ch 1, half corner of 3 dc in last sp, ch 2, sl st in top of starting ch 3.

Rnd 4: Ch 3, work half corner of 3 dc in corner sp, ch 1, * 3 dc in next ch-1 sp, ch 1, repeat from * to corner sp, work corner of 3 dc, ch 2, 3 dc in corner sp, ch 1. Repeat from first * twice, work 3 dc, ch 1 in each ch-1 sp to next corner sp, work half corner of 3 dc, ch 2, join with sl st in top of first st.

Rnd 5: Ch 3, 2 dc in joining sl st (half corner), ch 1, work from first * on rnd 4.

Rnd 6: Repeat rnd 4.

Rnd 7: Repeat rnd 4 and fasten off.

Rnd 8: With B, rep rnd 5 eight times.

Rnd 16: With C, rep rnd 5 eight times.

Rnd 24: With A, rep rnds 4 and 5 eight times.

Rnd 32: With B, rep rnds 4 and 5 eight times.

Rnd 40: With C, rep rnds 4 and 5 eight times.

Rnd 48: With A, repeat rnds 4 and 5 twice. Fasten off.

Finish: Run in all yarn ends on wrong side. Work one row of sc with A around outside edge.

This baby's blanket is warm and fluffy and is made with a ply of mohair and worsted. You can use a mohair blend such as Bernat's Venetian or Phildar's Anouchka or Dedicace.

The border is created with small granny squares, and the same pattern is repeated in the two large squares that make up the main part of the blanket. The decorative roses, made of worsted, add a contrasting touch.

Materials: Bernat's Berella knitting worsted 4-oz. skeins—4 skeins pink, 12 skeins mohair (not necessary, but makes the blanket softer and more luxurious—Bernat's Venetian #9517 Ash of Roses used here), 2 skeins worsted blue.

Hook: Size I

Gauge: 1 border square = 5½ inches
       1 center square = 16½ inches

Directions

Main squares: (Make 2.) You will be working with one strand worsted and one strand mohair.

Beg at center, ch 6. Join with sl st to form ring.

Rnd 1: Ch 3, work 2 dc in ring (ch 3, 3 dc shell in ring) 3 times; ch 3. Join with sl st to top of ch 3.

Sl st in next 2 dc, sl st in next space.

Rnd 2: Ch 3, in same sp work 2 dc, ch 3, and 3 dc (first corner)* ch 1, in next corner sp work 3 dc, ch 3, and 3 dc (another corner). Repeat from * twice more, ch 1, join with sl st to top of ch-3. Sl st in next 2 dc, sl st in next sp.

Rnd 3: Work a first corner in same sp *(ch 1, shell in next ch-1 sp), rep from * across to next corner, work corner, rep (ch 1, shell) to corner, repeat corner, rep (ch 1, shell) to corner, repeat corner, rep (ch 1, shell) to first corner.

Join with sl st top of ch 3.

Rnds 4 through 12: Continue with main color until 12 rounds have been completed. Fasten off.

Border squares: Make 22. Using contrasting color, blue, ch 4 and join into a ring with a sl st into first ch.

Rnd 1: *Ch 2, 4 dc into ring, sl st into ring, rep from * 3 times more.

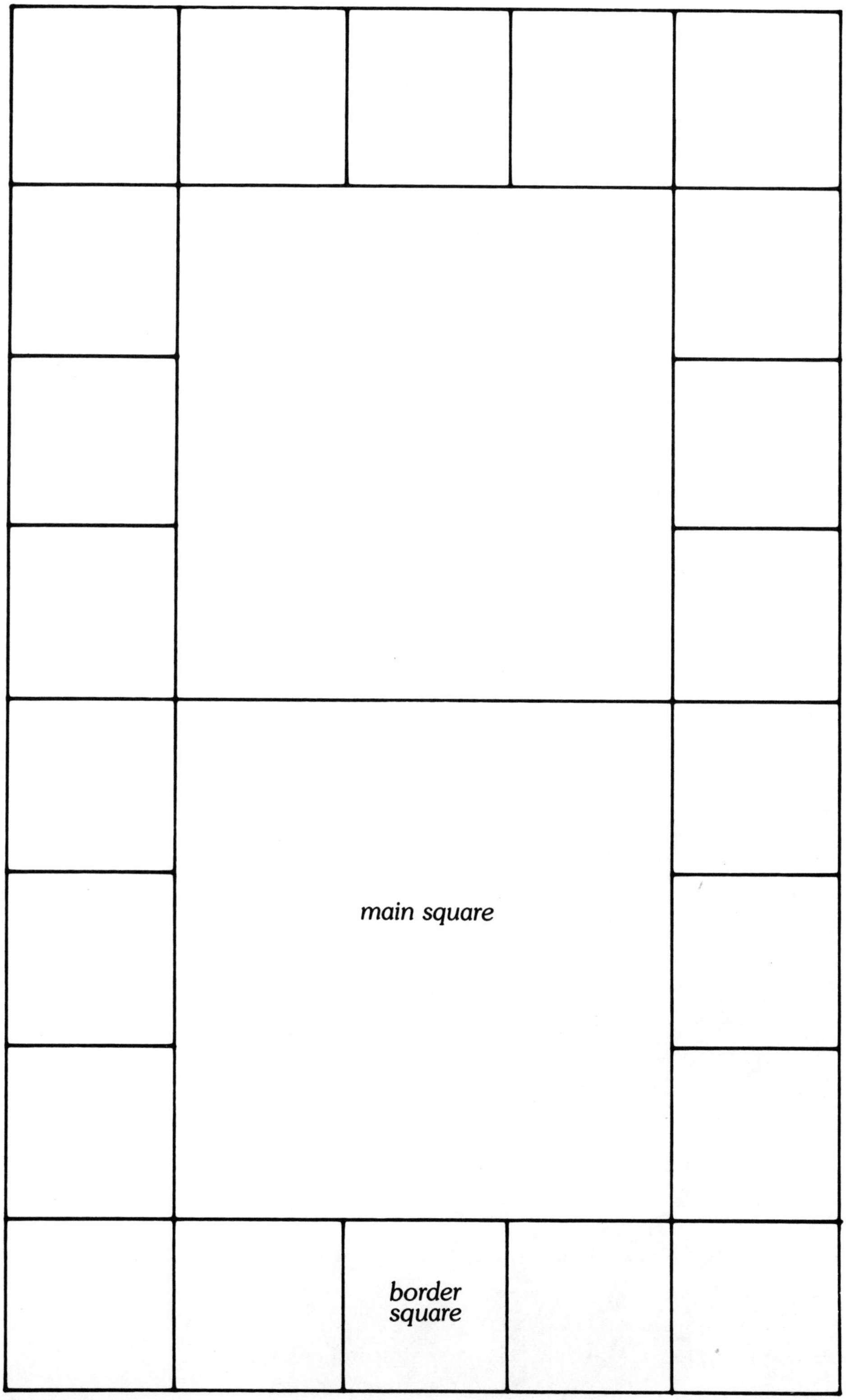

main square

border
square

Assembly diagram

Rnd 2: Sl st into back of 3rd dc, * keeping yarn at back of work, ch 4, sl st into back of 3rd dc of next grp, rep from * twice more, ch 4, join with a sl st first sl st.

Rnd 3: Into each sp work 1 sl st, 5 dc, 1 sl st.

Rnd 4: * 6 ch, 1 sl st into back of sl st bet petals, rep from * 3 times more. Attach main color.

Rnd 5: Ch 3 (2 dc, 3 ch, 3 dc) into same sp, * 1 ch (3 dc, 3 ch, 3 dc) into next sp, rep from * twice more, 1 ch, join with a sl st to 3rd of first 3-ch.

Rnd 6: Ch 3 (2 dc, 3 ch, 3 dc) into same sp, *1 ch, 3 dc into 1 ch sp, 1 ch (3 dc, 3 ch, 3 dc) into 3 ch sp, rep from * twice more, 1 ch, 3 dc into 1 ch sp, 1 ch, join with a sl st to 3rd of first 3-ch.

Rnd 7: Ch 3 (2 dc, 3 ch, 3 dc) into same sp, *(1 ch, 3 dc into 1 ch sp) twice, 1 ch (3 dc, 3 ch, 3 dc) into 3 ch sp, rep from * twice more (1 ch, 3 dc into 1 ch sp) twice, 1 ch, join with a sl st to 3rd of first 3-ch.
Fasten off.

Finish: Using main yarn, sew large squares tog or attach with sc. Attach all small squares around outside edge, and single crochet around entire blanket edges. See diagram for placement of squares.

Soft baby coverlet

This soft, ice-cream colored afghan is made of 4-ply acrylic and is completely washable. The coverlet will keep any baby warm and snug on a carriage outing.

The finished afghan is 38×50 inches.

Materials: Dupont 100% Acrilon 4-ply weight 3-oz. balls—3 balls each of pink and blue; 4 balls of white.
Hook: H

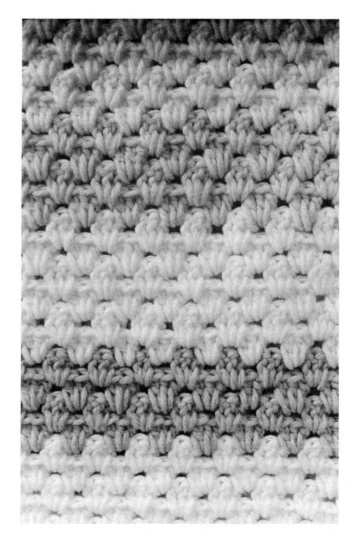

Soft baby coverlet

Directions

With blue yarn, loosely crochet a chain 38 inches long.

Row 1: 3 dc in first st. Skip next ch st. Continue with 3 dc, sk 1 st to end of row. At end of row, sc 1 ch st and turn.

Row 2: Work in the space between each of the pattern stitches. 3 dc, sc next space, and continue to end of row. Sc 1 and turn.

Continue for 4 rows of blue, change for 6 rows of white, 4 rows of pink, 6 rows white, 4 rows blue, etc. until piece measures 50 inches long.

Finish: Sc with blue around entire edge

Pram pillow

The matching pillow adds a nice touch to carriage or crib and is worked the same as for coverlet. Finished size is 12×14 inches.

The color pattern is as follows: 2 rows blue, 1 row white, 2 rows pink. Make 2 and stitch together with sc around edges. Stuff with Polyfil or pillow form before completely closing 4th side.

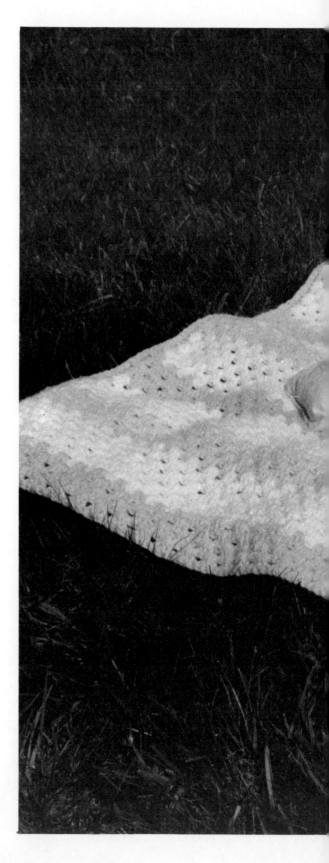

Apple granny

This traditional granny afghan reminds me of ripe red and green granny apples. It's crisp and delicious looking and easy to make. And just for a change of pace, the center is banana colored.

It won't take long to finish this project, which is made up of twenty 16×16-inch squares. The finished afghan measures 68×84 inches.

Materials: Bernat Berella knitting worsted or Bernat Sesame wool 4-oz. skeins—5 skeins each of pale yellow banana (A) and scarlet (B); 6 skeins of rose (C); 12 skeins of medium olive green (D).
Hook: H
Gauge: 2 rnds = 1 inch

Directions

Square: With A, ch 5, join with sl st to form a ring.
Rnd 1: Ch 3, 2 dc in ring, * ch 3, 3 dc in ring, repeat from * twice, end ch 3, sl st in 3rd st of ch-3.
Rnd 2: Sl st to first lp, ch 3 (2 dc, ch 3, 3 dc) in same lp (corner); * ch 1, sk 3 dc (3 dc, ch 3, 3 dc) in next lp, rep from * twice, and ch 1, sl st in top of ch-3.
Rnd 3: Sl st to corner lp, ch 3 (2 dc, ch 3, 3 dc) in

same lp; * ch 1, 3 dc in next lp, ch 1, 3 dc, ch 3, 3 dc in corner lp, rep from *, end ch 1, 3 dc in next lp, ch 1, sl st in top of ch-3.

Rnd 4: Sl st to corner lp, ch 3 (2 dc, ch 3, 3 dc) in same lp; * ch 1, 3 dc in first lp, ch 1, 3 dc in 2nd lp, ch 1, 3 dc, ch 3, 3 dc in corner lp, rep from *, end ch 1 (3 dc in lp) twice, ch 1, sl st in top of ch-3.

Continue working as for rnd 4 having 1 more dc group on each side every rnd. After 4 rnds A, work 4 rnds B, 4 rnds C, 4 rnds D—16 rnds in all. To change colors, begin new color in a corner lp.

Finish: Sew together 5 rows of 4 squares each.

Border: Single crochet 1 row of green all around.

Rnd 2: Dc all around.

Rnd 3: With red, hdc all around.

Rnd 4: With green, hdc all around.

A field of daisies

Fresh as springtime, the overall daisy pattern is made up of familiar crocheted granny squares. This design is a favorite with most crocheters. You can create it as shown here, with a background of blue, or you might prefer to set your daisies in a field of green as if growing on a lawn.

Made of 4-ply washable orlon, the finished afghan is 48 × 64 inches. You can, of course, alter the size by adding or subtracting motifs.

Materials: Coats & Clark Wintuk 3½-oz. skeins—5 skeins yellow (A), 20 skeins white (B), 20 skeins blue (C).
Hook: G
Gauge: 7dc = 2 inches

Directions

Make 192. With color A, ch 4, join with sl st to form ring.
Rnd 1: Ch 3 (counts as 1 sc and ch 1), * sc in center of ring, ch 1, repeat from * 4 times, join with sl st to 2nd ch of starting ch.
Rnd 2: * (sc, ch 1, sc) in next ch-1 sp, repeat from * 5 times, join with sl st to first sc. Break off color A.
Rnd 3: Attach color B to any sc, ch 4, keeping last lp of each st on hook, 2 dbl tr in same sc, yo and draw thru 3 lps on hook, ch 3, * keeping last lp on each st on hook, 3 dbl tr in next sc, yo and draw through 4 lps on hook, ch 3, rep from * 10 times, join with sl st to tip of first petal—12 petals. Break off color B.
Rnd 4: Attach color C (blue) to any ch-3 sp, ch 3 (3 dc, ch 2, 4 dc) in same sp (first corner), * (4 dc in next ch-3 sp) 2 times (4 dc, ch 2, 4 dc) in next ch-3 sp, repeat from * (4 dc in next 3-ch sp) 2 times, join with sl st to top of starting ch.
Finish: With C, sew 12 motifs across and 16 down. With B, work 3 rnds of sc around afghan, working sc, ch 1, sc in corner sps. Join each rnd with sl st. Fasten off.

A field of daisies

Source list

If you have trouble obtaining any of the yarns specified for the projects, you can write to the following addresses for information on mail-order sources or for the name of a store in your area that carries the material.

If you have any problems, suggestions, or experiences to share concerning your craftwork, drop me a note at the studio in Nantucket.

Leslie Linsley
Main Street
Nantucket, Massachusetts 02554

Bernat Yarn and Craft Corp.
Uxbridge, Massachusetts 01569

Bucilla Yarns
150 Meadowlands Parkway
Secaucus, New Jersey 07094

Christopher Sheep Farm
Richmond, Maine 04103

Coats & Clark
75 Rockefeller Plaza
New York, New York 10019

Phildar, Inc.
6438 Dawson Boulevard
Norcross, Georgia 30093

The Settlement Farm
Irish Settlement Road
R.F.D. 1
Box 540
Cambridge, Vermont 05444

Tahki Imports Ltd.
92 Kennedy Street
Hackensack, New Jersey 07601

Mail order for Phildar yarns

Creative Needles
436 Avenue of the Americas
New York, New York 10011

Make your home special

Since 1922, millions of men and women have turned to *Better Homes and Gardens* magazine for help in making their homes more enjoyable places to be. You, too, can trust *Better Homes and Gardens* to provide you with the best in ideas, inspiration and information for better family living.

In every issue you'll find ideas on food and recipes, decorating and furnishings, crafts and hobbies, remodeling and building, gardening and outdoor living plus family money management, health, education, pets, car maintenance and more.

For information on how you can have *Better Homes and Gardens* delivered to your door, write to: Mr. Robert Austin, P.O. Box 4536, Des Moines, IA 50336.

Better Homes and Gardens®

The Idea Magazine for Better Homes and Families

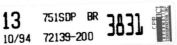